How to
MAKE YOUR OWN
LURES AND FLIES

How to
MAKE YOUR OWN
LURES AND FLIES

Mel Marshall

Photographs by the author
and Aldine Marshall

OUTDOOR LIFE ● FUNK & WAGNALLS
New York

Times Mirror Magazines, Inc.
Book Division

Editor and Publisher	John W. Sill
Executive Editor	Henry Gross
Associate Editor	Neil Soderstrom
Art Director	Jeff Fitschen
Production Manager	Millicent La Roque
Editorial Assistants	Pat Blair
	Ellen Patrisso

Library of Congress Catalog Card Number: 76-014674
Funk & Wagnalls Hardcover Edition: ISBN 0-308-10290-8
Paperback Edition: ISBN 0-308-10292-4

Second Printing, 1977

ACKNOWLEDGMENTS

Special thanks for special help to Bob Reed and William Barlow, C. Bendfeldt and Jack Walworth, Rich Miller and Harold Eddins, Bob McDonald and Joe Barkley, Don Ormson and Robert Wilson, and Woody Wood.

Manufactured in the United States of America

Contents

Introduction

Nobody knows just how ancient the art of taking fish on artificial lures and flies really is.

Egyptian tomb hieroglyphics dated only as having been inscribed "before 3500 B.C." show anglers casting shell and bronze lures with both rods and handlines, and in most of the world's waters, bare-hook lures of bone and shell are known to have been used by primitive man in the days before history began to be written.

Around the year 2000 B.C., a Greek naturalist named Claudius Aelianus wrote what must be the first detailed step-by-step description of how an artificial fly was tied. Because later writers used Aelianus's works as source material, his description of the fly modern anglers call the Red Hackle is often attributed to others.

A question you might fairly ask at this point is: "After such a long time, during which so many books have been written about lures and flies, why should another one be necessary?" The best answer is a story.

In 1931, the president of a firm that was then a leader in automobile manufacturing resigned his job. In his resignation statement, he said: "There are no more challenges in designing and making motor cars. The automobile has now reached such a state of perfection that further improvements are not merely unlikely, they are impossible."

Each year sees new materials added to the list of those traditionally used in lure making and fly tying; each year new lures appear, new fly patterns are created. Each year more fishermen take up the craft of making their own lures and flies and look for information about materials and techniques.

Is there any better reason for a new book on lures and flies?

M. M.

1

HOW TO
MAKE LURES

1

How Lures Began

JUST EXACTLY WHEN anglers discovered that fish would strike an artificial lure must remain veiled in the mists of the past. The first time that artificial lures appear in written history is in the *Halieutica,* the first extensive book about fishing, written by the Greek author-naturalist Oppian about 160 A.D.

Almost all early explorers who left records of their ventures into unknown regions note that primitive peoples living in widely separated geographical areas used artificial lures, most often made from bone or shell. Fishhooks of bone and stone were used as early as 3500 B.C., hooks of metal as early as 1000 B.C., and before hooks were made lures were fitted with a gorge, a sliver of bone or hardwood sharpened at each end and pierced in the center for a length of tough sinew. Attached by this sinew to a lure, the gorge caught crosswise in the mouth or gullet of a fish hitting the lure.

In its early days, lure fishing was a matter of trailing the lure behind a boat, or wading out into the surf to cast it with a bobbin or shuttle, using a line of vines or thin strips of hide. In later years, lines woven of horsehair were used. Inland, the lure was dangled in the current of a river, perhaps dragged through the water by the fisherman as he walked along the bank.

Rods first appeared in the 12th century, but reels were not developed for another 500 years. Even after reels were adopted, a fisherman's cast was usually limited to twice the length of his rod, since rigid guides that would allow the coarse lines of the day to run through them were not invented until around 1790. Most early rods were 14 to 16 feet long, so a good cast was about 30 feet.

Trollers were better off than fishermen who cast their lures. Even the clumsy reels — little more than spools of wood grooved to hold the line, and called "winches" — allowed the troller to pay out line back of a boat. The wobbling spoon predominated as a lure; the first revolving-blade lure, the Devon Minnow, was a frustrating device with a bullet-shaped body and blades like wings. The lure revolved in only one direction, and when used any length of time it twisted and kinked lines beyond restoration, so Devon

Minnows were sold in pairs. One of the pair revolved to the right, the other to the left, and after one had been used for a half-hour or so, it was changed for its counter-turning twin, which untwisted the kinked line. When the line began to twist in the opposite direction, the first minnow was put back on. The free-spinning swivel that today avoids kinked lines was unknown until late in the 19th century.

Lure fishing became both practical and popular in the mid-1800s. In 1806 George Snyder, a Kentucky watchmaker, had built himself a reel out of clock parts, to use in casting minnows from a boat into the shoreline bushes where bass were lurking. The reel was delicate, and its clock gears bent and broke under strain, but the gearing made it possible for fishermen to retrieve line quickly, and the news of the invention spread. About 1820, another watchmaker, Jonathan Meek, got hold of one of Snyder's reels and improved it with sturdier gears. A few years later still another fisherman, Benjamin Milam, made further improvements to the original handmade reel, and Milam put his version into commercial production in the late 1820s.

By the 1840s, baitcasting reels were being widely used, but lures were scarce. The most popular were spoons, called "spoon-hooks" in those days. Angling legend attributes discovery of the spoon to a Connecticut dentist, Dr. Thomas J. Buell. The story goes that Buell and his family were returning from a day of picnicking on the shores of a lake near their home, and as the good doctor was rowing the party back across the lake in the evening dusk, one of the youngsters tossed a spoon from the lunch basket into the water. Buell, watching the spoon swaying rhythmically as it sank, saw a big bass rise from the depths and gulp in the shining bit of metal. Inspired by this, the doctor later sawed the handles off some of his wife's teaspoons, drilled holes in them for hooks and a line eye and cleared out the lunker bass from all the lakes in the neighborhood. It's a good story and might even be true.

Although the wobbling spoon-type lure was a few centuries old in the days when Buell lived, he gets credit for putting "spoon-hooks" on the market, for in 1815 he patented them and began manufacturing them commercially. To avoid conflict with Buell's patent, others began making spoons of different shapes, and for the next seventy-five or eighty years, spoons were the predominant casting lure.

In 1897, a Michigan fisherman named Jim Heddon decided that the minnow-shaped lures he'd been whittling experimentally from cedar "plugs" were worth patenting. Unknown to Heddon, another Michigander, J. T. Lowe, had been working along similar lines and had reached the same conclusion Heddon arrived at, and at about the same time. Patent applications for Heddon's "Dowgiac" lure and Lowe's "Tango" plug arrived at the U.S. Patent Office in Washington on the same day. Either Heddon's papers were delivered in an earlier mail, or they were opened and recorded first; at any rate, the first patent for an elongated cylindrical wooden lure was awarded to him.

Heddon began manufacturing his lure soon after the patent was granted; Lowe, in spite of his lack of patent protection, also put his lure on the market, and others followed quickly. These prototypes of today's big family of thick-bodied lures—as opposed to thin-bodied metal lures—proved the ideal complements to the Snyder-Meek-Milam reels. Unlike metal lures, which sank fast, the wooden plugs could be retrieved very slowly, and at controlled depths. Within a short time, manufacturers learned to build depth controls into their lures by slanting the lures in front or by equipping them with fins or rudders. For the first half of the 20th century, the plug and the revolving-spool reel dominated North American angling.

Unnoticed by American fishermen, things were happening in Europe during that half-century. Sometime around 1900, a British cottonmill operator, Alfred Holden Illingworth, noticed the way cotton threads flowed under minimum tension off the tops of spinning bobbins in his mill. Illingworth saw the principle for a new kind of fishing reel—new, at least, to him, for primitive anglers of earlier centuries had spooled their lines on a bobbin or shuttle equipped with a short grip and had learned to cast so that the lure's weight pulled the line off the end of the bobbin in loose spirals.

By 1905, Illingworth had worked out a usable reel and put it into commercial production; the derivation of the name "spinning reel" is obvious. This first reel lacked two major developments that were to be added later: the bail pickup was created by Hardy's reel designers in the 1930s, and the eccentric cam on the spool shaft that moves the spool back and forth so that the line will crosswind was the work of Charles Ritz of the hotel family in the 1940s. Before these improvements, the line on a spinning reel had to be freed for casting and guided back into the pickup roller by hand, and the fixed position of the spool on early reels made piling-up or packing-up of lines almost inevitable, resulting in snarls and birdcages during the cast.

These digressions into reel developments aren't frivolous; in modern lure fishing the lure and rod are interdependent. Early reels with revolving spools did not have the adjustments that give today's reels their versatility. Not too many years ago, very heavy lures were needed to pull line off a revolving-spool reel, and the lure maker had to take this limiting factor into consideration in his plans. Until the post–World War II era, spool tension adjustments and free-spooling on freshwater reels were features generally confined to reels made for tournament casters. The first really flexible reel I owned was a Shakespeare model of the 1930s, and to adjust spool tension it was necessary to use oils of different viscosity when switching from $3/8$- to $5/8$-ounce plugs. Freed from weight problems, the lure maker of today, whether professional or amateur, not only has a wider range of choice in materials but has a whole world of substances and forms that were not available to those of earlier days.

Today's lure maker can strike out into new designs and patterns without the inhibitions of his predecessors for another reason, too. Fishermen have finally learned that a successful lure need not be a slavish representation of a living form of aquatic life. We know that simulation is as effective as imitation, and when we want to imitate, we have new plastics that reproduce not only the living look but also the living feel of the water-life on which game fish feed.

Of course, no fisherman knows with any real certainty how his lure looks to a fish, what the lure resembles in the brain or instincts of a bass or trout, or what really motivates the fish to strike. If we knew this, much of the challenge of fishing would be lost, and all the challenge of creating new lures. For instance, about the time this book was started, plugs imitating miniature beer cans came on the market, and fishermen using them report that they're as successful as a lot of plugs that look like natural minnows. Every angler has heard about, and most have experienced, the phenomenon of fish striking even unlikelier objects than beer can-shaped plugs.

When pull-tab beer cans first appeared, reports came in from lakes all over the land that fish caught and cleaned were found to be full of the pull-tabs tossed overboard by boaters. Somehow, in ways still mysterious to us, strange bits and pieces of metal, cloth, plastic, or wood either appear to the fish as food, perhaps a new substance that might possibly be edible, or as an intruder that inspires anger and causes the fish to strike at it.

This opens a very wide door to the amateur lure maker. It encourages him to experiment beyond simply assembling kits made up of components that have been tried and tested. Unfettered by the commercial requirements of manufacturers, who must produce in volume lures that will attract fishermen as well as fish, the amateur can strike out into new fields of form and action, use new materials and oddball designs, in creating lures for his own pleasure.

Certainly there's nothing wrong with assembling kits, if you're after tested patterns plus economy and variety. Simply by screwing a few hook eyes into a preformed lure body and perhaps applying a coat or two of enamel, you can save from 50 to 75 percent of the cost of your lures. By going a step further, your savings are even greater. A little time and effort and a reasonable skill with common hand tools applied to creating your own lures from scratch allow you to produce for pennies virtually the same lures that sell for dollars. As this is being written, few lures sell for less than $1.00 across the store counter, and most of them are in the $1.50 to $2.50 range. A kit will allow you to assemble these lures for 60¢ to 70¢ each, and working from scratch you can produce them for 20¢ to 35¢ each plus your time.

Contrary to what you might think, you don't need a factory full of punches and presses to form metal lures, using dies you can make yourself. Nor do you need a battery of automated lathes to produce wooden plugs, as long as you own a knife and a file or two and can invest in a few sheets of sandpaper. If you presently lack skill in using tools, the skill will develop as you work—after all, did you make a perfect cast the first time you picked up a rod and reel?

Perhaps your productions won't be as perfect as the lures that come out of a factory, but how important is that to the fish? Nor do you need to know anything about aquadynamics, the complicated computations that deal with the behavior of various shapes in and under water. These are useful to designers interested in producing shapes with a predictable action, but all you really need to know is that any form of any material lighter than such heavy metals as lead will move in an erratic fashion unless it is a spheroid or ovoid.

Freely translated, this simply means that if you drop a flat shape into water it will not sink in a perfectly straight line, even if it is attached to a cord by which it is being pulled. There are the mathematical formulas just mentioned that can be used to calculate the behavior of shapes having different curvatures and contours, but all you really need to know is that any flat metal or heavy plastic will zig and zag when pulled underwater. The fascination of lure making is experimenting with different contours and curves as you try to find one that will move in a manner that interests fish. If you know this in advance, you might as well buy your lures ready-made.

The first half of this book is concerned with lure making. Those who prefer to fish with flies instead of lures or who divide their angling activities between these two methods of fishing will find information about flies in the book's second part.

2

Lure Families

LURES CAN BE DIVIDED into three large families. Because they came first, the thin-bodied lure family leads our list. Into this family grouping go all lures made of metal and such materials as shell or plastic pressed into thin configurations. This means that the thin-bodied lure family embraces spoons, wobblers, darters, and spinners, even those spinners that have some kind of a body behind them, or those that are part of an assembly including a fur- or feather-covered hook.

Into family number two go all thick-bodied lures: plugs made from wood or hard plastic, regardless of their weight, shape, or size. These lures are generally cylindrical or oval in shape and may be formed by carving wood or molding nonresilient plastic.

The third family, the newest in the field, takes in all lures formed of soft, resilient plastics; these can be grouped under the descriptive term, soft-bodied lures. The lures in this family almost always imitate with more or less detail and precision some species of underwater amphibian or insect, such as salamanders, crayfish, grubs, worms, frogs, and so on. Soft plastic lures simulating minnows will be included in this family, although they might properly be classified with the thick-bodied group. Our soft-bodied lure family will also include another borderline case in the form of lures made of surgical rubber or commercial plastic tubing, even if these lures have a hard jig head cast of metal.

Some overlapping is inevitable; just as human families intermingle, so do the families of lures. Some soft-bodied lures may include a tiny spoon or spinner, just as some of the lures in the thin-bodied family may have feathers or fur in their make-up.

It should be borne in mind that we're not going to be concerned in any way with the method you choose to use in getting a lure out to where a fish can see it. We're concerned here only with making lures, not with the style or kind of tackle you employ in fishing.

Having established our families, let's look at their individual members. All three of the families are big ones, so big that it's impossible to examine each lure in each family by its trade or formal name. We'll therefore try to pick out prototypes characteristic of the lures in the three families, and perhaps in some cases identify them by a trade name with which a given family member is closely or generally associated.

Nobody has ever counted the total number of lures available, but it runs into the tens of thousands. A major tackle manufacturer, for instance, will list in his catalog a basic line of perhaps thirty to fifty thick-bodied lures, each of which is available in three or four sizes and twenty or twenty-five finishes. This runs up to about 5,000 thick-bodied lure variations, and in the same catalog this manufacturer will also list a couple of dozen thin-bodied lures, each available in several sizes and a multitude of finishes. It's going to take a braver man than me to try to list all the different lures available today.

THIN-BODIED LURES

Thin-bodied lures can be subdivided into three categories: wobblers, darters, and spinners. Into the wobbler group go all the spoons that can best be described as concave metal shapes, usually oval, with a hook on one end, the line on the other, and which are basically one-piece, having neither shafts nor bodies. Most of these lures have a sort of tipsy, lurching action when they're being retrieved, like the gait of a New Year's Eve reveler.

Darters, on the other hand, have a quick, uncertain action as they're retrieved. They zigzag like a hound dog trying to pick up a lost scent. Gener-

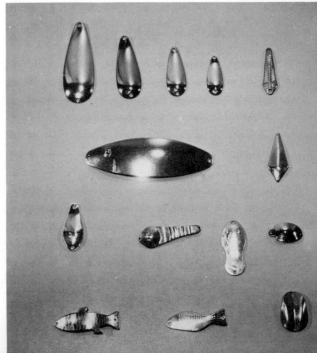

Wobblers and darters, two types of thin-bodied lures, are bodiless; hook and line are attached to them directly.

Spinners, another thin-bodied lure group, include such lures as the Colorado spinners, top left; the Indiana and Willow Leaf spinners just below them; and the bodied spinning lures of the Mepps-Abu type, which have a variety of blade shapes. At right are spinners that are strung together to make trolling lures.

ally nervous and fluttery rather than lazy and rhythmic, darters resemble wobblers only in their construction, in that they're bodiless, and both hook and line are attached to them directly.

Spinners are the biggest and most varied of the thin-bodied lure family. With very rare exceptions, they're attached to a shaft of some kind by a clevis, which is a C-shaped piece of metal with its ends drilled out to accomodate the shaft, generally a length of wire. A spinner may be nothing but blade, shaft, and hook, or it may be dolled up with beads strung on the shaft, or it may have a solid or sectioned body of some kind. The hook may be bare, or covered with fur or feathers, or ornamented with a bit of colored plastic tubing. Then there are the trolling lures, which are simply a number of spinners on a series of interconnected shafts.

Prototype lures that can be considered typical of each of these families are the Eppinger Daredevle and Johnson Spoon for the wobblers, the Martin Panther and Gladding SuperDuper for the darters, the traditional Colorado Spinner, the Mepps, the Abu Reflex, and the Doc Shelton for the spinner family.

In spite of the variety of shapes, sizes, and finishes that characterize lures of the thin-bodied family, there are few that you cannot duplicate on your own workbench, using the simplest standard tools. If you want to confine your work to only the simplest procedures, you can buy factory-made components for all these lures and just assemble them. However, if you want to enjoy the greatest savings by putting in a bit more work, you can very readily fabricate your own spoon and spinner blades, often from scrap materials costing little or nothing.

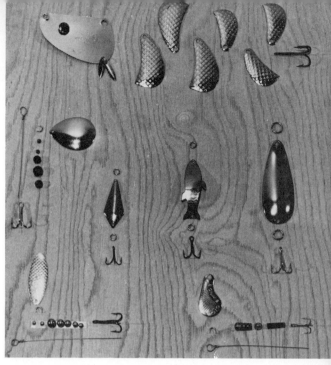

A typical kit from which thin-bodied lures can be assembled includes the components required to put together one or more complete lures.

At prices current while this is being written, assembling the average wobbling or darting lure will cost you between 12¢ and 35¢ for the blade, depending on its size and the source from which you buy, 8¢ to 12¢ for the hook, and about ½¢ to 1¢ for connecting rings, so lures in this group will range in cost from about 21¢ to 48¢; less, if you buy blades and hooks in quantity. Lures in the spinner group will total only from 18¢ to 24¢ for plain-shafted spinners to 25¢ to 35¢ for spinners of the body-shafted type. If you decide to go all-out and form your own blades, your costs will be cut to the expense of hooks alone.

THICK-BODIED LURES

Ancestors of the thick-bodied lure family were, as we've noted, the ancient Devon Minnow and Jim Heddon's cedar plug. From them have descended a numerous brood, varied beyond the dreams of anglers who used these ancestor lures.

Plugs are the dominant member of this branch of the lure family, and while today many plugs are molded from tough, high-impact plastics, the wooden plug is still with us, and still very healthy. New enamel finishes, based on epoxy and acrylic materials, have actually given new life to the wooden plug.

Almost without exception, thick-bodied lures are designed to imitate minnows or other small fish. They are generally classified as floaters or divers and are often equipped with scoops or rudders that help them stay on the surface or run underwater, sometimes at predetermined depths.

13

Plugs dominate the thick-bodied lure family. Typical well-known commercial lures like these can be duplicated by assembling kits or forming your own lure bodies.

Some floating plugs have plates that create a splashing on the water; typical of these are the Arbogast Jitterbug and the Heddon Crazy Crawler. Floating plugs made of plastic usually have hollow bodies, while those designed to run deep may be weighted in the body cavity. One group is designed to give off a high-frequency noise underwater as an attraction to cruising game fish.

Perhaps the most distinguishing characteristic of thick-bodied lures is not their shape, but the wide range of color finishes they display. Most of the rainbow spectrum of finishes offered by manufacturers can be duplicated by some experimental mixing of paint or enamel.

Components for thick-bodied lures can be bought in kit form or individually. A typical plug assembly kit will contain unpainted or painted bodies together with all the hooks and hardware necessary to assemble the plugs. Usually, such kits contain parts for a half-dozen lures and sell for $5.00 to $7.00, with kits containing unpainted bodies costing somewhat less. Your cost per assembled plug, based on averaging prices from several supply sources, will run from 83¢ to $1.25 for prepainted plugs, and from 75¢ to $1.25 if you buy the unpainted body kits. Actually, the kits with the painted bodies are your best buy, unless you're planning to use up leftover paints that you have on hand, because if you don't want all your painted plugs to look alike, you'd spend more than the difference in the kit costs buying several shades of paint for the finishing job.

Buying unassembled components is much less costly. Plug bodies range from 18¢ to 32¢ each, depending on source and size, the hardware such as hook eyes will add about 2¢ to the cost per plug, and hooks will add 24¢ to 30¢, since most thick-bodied lures require two and often three hooks. Paint

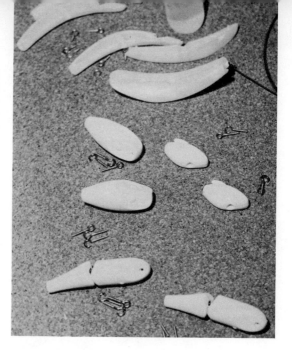

Like the kits already mentioned for thin-bodied lures, those that produce thick-bodied lures include all body shapes and hardware, but usually you'll be expected to furnish the paint.

adds another penny or two. Your cost per lure will range, then, from 45¢ to 65¢ if you choose to go this route.

Far and away your best bet, if your primary interest is saving money, is to form your own plug bodies. If you insist on using the traditional basswood, you can buy blanks for 4¢ to 6¢ each; basswood is a nice wood with which to work, responsive to tools, without crazy graining, and easy to finish. However, a casual friendly visit to a construction site or to a cabinet shop will usually produce all the scrap lumber you can use—at no cost whatever. This pulls your cost down to the 28¢ to 36¢ you'll invest in paint, hardware, and hooks for each plug—plus the time you put in forming and finishing bodies.

SOFT-BODIED LURES

While this family of lures in the form of rubber-based cast forms has been around for a long time, it spurted into sudden popularity during the 1960s, when soft plastic replaced rubber as a molding material. This not only made it possible for the fisherman favoring these lures to cast his own but reduced casting costs drastically, since battered, chewed-up lures can be remelted and remolded.

Generally, worms are the most popular soft-bodied lure shapes, though salamanders—often called "waterdogs" or "water puppies"—and crayfish, frogs, and other shapes quickly appeared. All of the forms can be cast in just about any shade required, from translucent or "natural" to solid black, including two- and three-toned lures if the caster wants to be very fancy.

After the molded forms there appeared soft-bodied lures made from

15

rubber surgical tubing and from commercial plastic tubings. This sub-family may simply consist of a hook slipped inside a short piece of tubing or may be fitted back of a lead jig head. Since jig heads are available in a tremendous range of sizes and styles, you can build lures on them to serve the entire fishing spectrum from saltwater fish to panfish.

Fully assembled soft-bodied lures are beginning to appear in blister-packs as this is written. Usually each pack contains three to four lures of the same kind and is priced in the $1.75 to $2.00 range, which means that each lure costs from 40¢ to 50¢, depending on the packaging and lure sizes. Hooks and weights add another 10¢. Even if you include the cost of the molds, you can do a lot better by casting your own.

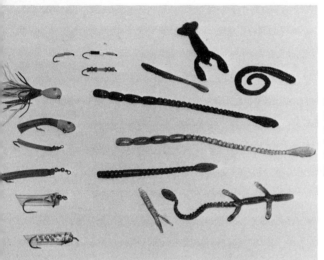

Soft-bodied lures include tube lures, at left, for which no kits are available, and cast plastic worms and other bait shapes, for which you can buy molds and casting materials.

Molds for casting plastic soft-bodied lures range in price from less than $1.00 for a one- or two-cavity worm mold to around $5.00 for multi-cavity molds that will produce nine or ten worms at one pouring. Other shapes, salamanders, crayfish, and so on, are priced from about $2.00 to $6.00, depending on size and complexity. The molds are infinitely reusable. No special equipment other than the molds is required, and the casting does not require extreme heat.

Plastic casting material costs from $1.75 to $2.00 a pint, depending on your supply source and the quantity you buy. A pint of the material will produce about fifty 8-inch worms. A 2-ounce bottle of dye, enough to color a gallon of material, costs around 60¢. If you feel inclined to make lures that are either softer or firmer than the standard casting material yields, modifiers cost about $1.50 a pint and are used at the ratio of an ounce to 10 ounces of the plastic material. If you cast fifty worms in a mold costing $2.50, your materials cost will be about 4½¢ per worm; add a penny or so

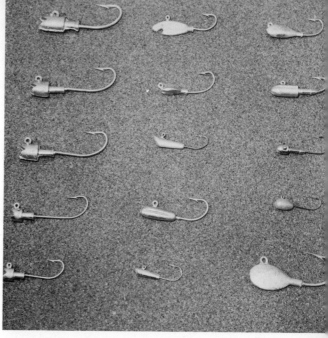

Jig heads for forming soft-bodied tube or skirted lures are made in a tremendous variety of shapes and sizes.

to amortize the cost of the mold, and after you've used the mold a half-dozen times, it's paid its way. Remember, too, that damaged, chewed-up lures can be remelted. Ultimately, you'll wind up with a cost of around 3¢ per worm.

Tubing lures will vary in cost depending on the quantity of tubing bought in a single purchase, and the fittings used. Bare-hook tubing lures will cost less than jig-head lures, of course. Rubber tubing runs from 16¢ to 28¢ per foot in 10-foot lengths, depending on your source of supply; plastic tubing costs about a third less. A foot of tubing will yield five to six bodies; add a penny for fittings and 4¢ to 5¢ for the hook, and your tube lures will come out at an overall average cost of less than 10¢ each.

If you head these lures with metal jigs, figure jig prices in the range of 8¢ to 14¢ each, depending on size and supplier, but subtract the hook cost from your total, since your jigs will be hooked. Painting the heads will add a penny to your cost, if you use a good grade of enamel made for application on jig lead. If you fit out jig heads with fur or feathers, the cost will be a bit less, since these materials are less expensive than tubing. Any way you figure, though, you come out far ahead when you make your own, even buying precast jig heads. If you decide to cast your own heads, you'll be faced with the purchase of molds and hooks, but the molds will soon be amortized, and you can scrounge around at service stations for discarded lead wheel-balancing weights, at print shops for old type metal, and at junkyards for scrap lead.

There's one more thing that needs to be mentioned. While it's true that 99.99 percent of all your lure making can be handled with simple tools, unless you have the tools already, you're faced with buying them. We'll look at tools and materials a bit more closely in the next chapter.

3

Tools and Supplies

BEFORE YOU LIFT a hand to start making a lure, decide exactly what your approach is going to be to this pleasant and rewarding but sometimes demanding craft. If you're going into it for the sheer pleasure of creating and exercising your ingenuity, or as a hobby to take your mind off the worries that may beset you, that's one thing. If you're planning to make lures as a means of having a better-stocked tacklebox at the lowest possible cost, that's another.

Under the first set of conditions, you'll treat your lure making as you would any other hobby that you take up for fun and recreation, and count anything you spend for tools and supplies as a leisure-time investment. If a certain process calls for a left-handed clampertoe crimper, you'll go out and buy one, even though it's a special-purpose tool that you might use only once or twice a year.

Under the second hypothetical set of circumstances, you'll keep a watchful eye on costs, realizing that overinvesting in single-use tools will quickly wipe out the saving you plan to make by producing your own lures. So, instead of going out and buying that mythical left-handed clampertoe crimper, you'll devote a bit of time and ingenuity figuring out how to do the job with the tools you have on hand. The work might not be as easy, it might take a little longer to complete, and the finished lure might not look factory-pretty, but the chances are that it'll work just as well.

Learning this cost me a bit when I first got into lure making during the 1940s. My interest in home-produced lures was created by the nature of steelhead fishing, in which I was beginning to get deeply involved. Up to the time I got hooked on steelhead, about 90 percent of my fishing hours had been spent with a fly rod on trout waters, but I quickly discovered that there are few purists on steelhead streams, because during the time these fish are making their winter spawning run the days of clear water are short and infrequent. Steelhead fishing is one way to get rid of any tackle hangups you might have, and to learn to switch from flies to lures to bait depending on water conditions.

18

If you've never sought this finest of all fighting fish in the rivers of the Pacific Northwest, perhaps I should explain that they are found in big streams for the most part, with fast-boiling currents and rocky bottoms, and that most of the time they travel within a foot of the river's bed. Until you learn to feel the shift of underwater currents, those streams can swallow a lure on every cast you make. Even after you think you've acquired the touch, you'll still find yourself doing the one cast–one lost lure routine when you're learning a new stretch of water.

A number of my friends who were initiating me into the steelhead fraternity either assembled their own lures or made them from scratch, so I was exposed to a lot of conversation about lure making. I'd been tying flies and building rods for a number of years, but at that time I'd never tried my hand at lures. There hadn't been much reason to. Lures then cost from 20¢ to 40¢ apiece, and a 50¢ lure was considered expensive. I hadn't been fishing before in water as lure-hungry as those steelhead rivers were, but I quickly learned that even at the day's prevailing lure prices, the cost of replacements becomes a big factor when you fish almost daily for several hours at a stretch.

When I did decide to get into lure making, I asked a lot of questions of the fellows who had more experience, and one of them gifted me with the piece of advice about the danger of overbuying on tools, which I passed on to you a few paragraphs ago. Maybe it will help you to do as I did: figure ways to use the tools I had instead of rushing out to buy a lot of specialized tools for lure making.

Assuming that you do a certain amount of maintenance work on your house, your yard, your car, or your boat, it's quite likely that you'll have just about everything you need to get started with lures. There are some special gadgets that make things easier, of course, but few of these are very expensive. Those that are essential are few in number.

For instance, you can spend $5.00 to $6.00 on a device that enables you to produce eyes in leader wire just by turning a crank, or you can spend a half-hour of practice doing the same job with a couple of pairs of pliers that are needed to do other jobs as well. Or, you can buy one of the several

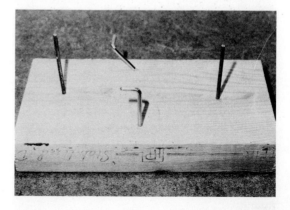

A homemade jig on which to form spinner shafts can be made in five minutes at a cost of less than 50¢

kinds of jigs that help you to get uniformity in shaft lengths, or for about 20¢ worth of nails and angle-screws plus a piece of scrap lumber you can make a jig that will do all these things and assist you in forming eyes as well. The jig in the picture took me less than ten minutes to make. All that's needed is to predrill pilot holes for the nails and angles, cut off the nailheads with wire cutters or a hacksaw and smooth them down with a file. We'll see later on how the jig is used.

Of course, if cost's no object, you can add a lot of extras. A jeweler's hand-held soft-jawed vise (and I don't own one) saves putting a protective strip of cloth or inner-tube rubber in the jaws of locking pliers when you're grinding or filing a lure blade. An etching pen allows you to inscribe patterns on a spinner or spoon blade and rub paint in the lines to give your blade more flash. If you need a bench anvil you can buy one—if you can find one—or you can pick up a short piece of railroad rail for a nickle or dime from a local scrapyard. Or, you can look around second-hand stores or garage sales for a burned-out electric iron that you can buy for 10¢ or 15¢, and make an anvil of its soleplate, as the accompanying pictures show.

If you want to go all the way, you can equip yourself with a home workshop-size electroplating outfit for around $40.00, or you can make dull lures shiny with metallic tapes at a cost of about 6¢ a blade. You can

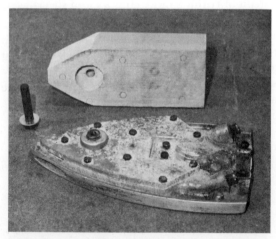

A burned-out electric iron makes a good bench anvil. The base can be shaped from any thick piece of scrap lumber, the hole for the one bolt needed to assemble it drilled and countersunk. The bolt is an SEA thread ³/₁₆ x 2 inches; thanks to standardization, it's used by all electric-iron makers. Assembled, the soleplate makes a very satisfactory bench anvil.

use aerosol cans when paint absolutely must be sprayed, or put in an airbrush outfit—$30.00—and the compressor needed to operate it—another $35.00. So, when you set about surveying the tool situation, do keep in mind that most commonplace everyday tools can and will do most of the jobs you need to perform in making lures.

From the tool lists that follow, you can cut your own pattern. I've divided them into two groups: essential tools, those that you really need, and luxuries that are useful but not really necessary.

For assembling thin-bodied lures from kits or components, the essential tools are:
   Longnose roundjaw pliers, often called lure-makers' pliers
   Flatjaw pliers
   Wire-cutting pliers
   Split-ring pliers—these allow you to put on split rings without splitting
      fingernails and fingertips

For making thin-bodied lures from scratch, the above tools plus:
   Electric drill (or drill press) with $\frac{1}{32}$, $\frac{1}{16}$, $\frac{1}{8}$ bits
   Ball-peen hammer
   Bench anvil—this was discussed above
   Jeweler's bag—this is a square leather bag about 6″ x 6″, filled with fine
      sand; mine was made by a shoe repairman and cost $2.00 when I
      had it made to use for the pictures that you'll see later on, so it's a
      current fair price
   Drill burrs, sometimes called rotary burrs; they cost about 50¢ each and
      come in several shapes, the oval and round ones being the most
      useful
   Shafted drill stones, similar to the bits, but finer-cutting; they, too, come
      in different shapes and cost about 50¢ each
   Grinding wheel, either a bench-type grinder or one that can be fitted
      with an arbor for use in an electric drill
   Vise—almost any kind will do
   Coping saw or jeweler's saw that will accept metal-cutting blades, and the
      necessary blades; I like the round blades coated with tungsten car-
      bide because they're virtually unbreakable and will cut through any-
      thing OR
   Electric saber saw or jig saw; a variable-speed model is a bonus
   Tinsnips OR a metal nibbling tool such as the Bernz
   Files—you can get by with one fine-cut file plus a small rat-tail file, but a
      coarse file such as a half-round mill bastard is a wise addition, and a
      warding file is a bonus

Useful, but not really necessary:
   Adjustable jaw-locking pliers, such as the ViseGrip
   Set of needle files
   Jeweler's soft-jawed hand vise

For assembling thick-bodied lures from kits or components, the essential tool is:
A pair of pliers — almost any kind will do

For making thick-bodied lures from scratch, the above plus:
Medium-cut woodworker's rasp
Craft knife with interchangeable blades, or any standard bench knife such as a Sloyd
Files — half-round mill bastard, flat or half-round fine-cut, triangular or knife fine-cut
Split-ring pliers
Wire-gauge drill bits — these are bits smaller than the $\frac{1}{32}''$ bits at which shop gauges end. The most useful sizes are #54, #55, and #56, which drill pilot holes for screw eyes
Vise

Useful, but not really necessary:
Power sander — you can do any sanding job by hand, but either an oscillating power sander or an arbor enabling you to use sanding disks in a drill will speed up jobs and save muscles for better purposes
SurForm tool, a Stanley woodworking device that helps when roughing in lure bodies

For assembling soft-bodied lures from components or kits:
None for molded forms, though a 75¢ worm sneller is a handy tool for fitting plastic lures with hooks

For assembling tube lures:
Split-ring pliers
Roundnose lure pliers
Craft knife or pocketknife

For making soft-bodied lures from scratch:
Molds — your choice of the shapes you use most often
Melting pot — any small metal pot; I use cheap tin cups
Heat source — if the boss of your kitchen objects to you using her range, use your camp stove in your workshop

If you're at all active in doing odd jobs around home, or if you do any kind of tackle tinkering, the chances are you'll have most of the necessary items as well as some of the useful but not essential tools. Those you're least likely to own are the lure pliers, the jeweler's bag, the drill burrs and stones, metal-cutting coping saw blades — incidentally, you can get by with a hacksaw, but a coping saw is a lot handier — and the tiny wire-gauge drill bits. Except for the split-ring pliers, which cost less than $1.00 and ought to be in every lure fisherman's tacklebox anyhow, these are all standard multiuse tools. If they're not among your workshop's equipment, most of them should be, and even if you buy them with lure making in mind, you'll find yourself using them for other jobs and wondering how you got along without them. How much they'll cost depends on how good you are at shopping for bargains.

KITS VS. COMPONENTS

Your next problem is one of materials. If you decide to limit yourself to assembling only, you'll have no problem at all, since every lure kit of the dozens I've looked at in preparing this book has been very complete, containing everything necessary—or at least, everything specified in the ads that offered them for sale. If you buy individual components, you're in for a session of catalog shopping and price comparison, but I've found that among the chief suppliers of tackle components, prices tend to balance out. An item that in one catalog is a bit higher will be offset in the next catalog by a slightly higher price on a different item.

However, you're almost going to be forced to shop by mail, unless you live in or near a large city where well-stocked tackle shops can be found. Most of us don't. The local suppliers we depend on simply can't generate enough sales volume for components to justify stocking them. The chances are your local purchases will be limited to such items as hooks and split rings. You'll find a list of suppliers in an appendix to this book, and in preparing it, I tested out most of them by placing orders. A few who advertised catalogs, either free or for a token fee, often refundable with your first purchase, didn't come through, and you won't find their names on the list. Uniformly, though, I got reasonably good service from all those from whom I ordered. The average time-lapse between order and delivery was three to four weeks, so don't expect overnight service if you live far from your supply sources. If your order isn't filled in four weeks, inquire.

Some of the catalogs, by the way, were very helpful. Those of Reed Tackle Company, Limit Manufacturing Company, Herter's, Netcraft, and E. Hille contain enough descriptive detail on the use of components so that even somebody totally unfamiliar with lures could order intelligently. One catalog, Reed's, went so far as to include parts lists for typical lures in a form that gives you at a glance the exact number, type, and size of components that you'd need, together with notes telling you why a certain component was essential to the lure's functioning.

Selecting components, then, is a matter of comparison shopping, if you want to buy every item at the very lowest price. On the basis of my own comparison shopping, you'll get uniformly good quality in the components you buy; just don't expect them to be finished in factory style. After all, that's part of your assembly job.

SCRAP METAL

If you're planning on forming your own blades and bodies, that's another matter. Don't let this idea of shaping spoon or spinner blades bug you, by

A Lure from a Spoon

1. Cut off the handle by striking it with a cold chisel.

2. Grind or file the cut spot until it is smooth.

3. Drill holes at each end to accommodate eye fittings.

24

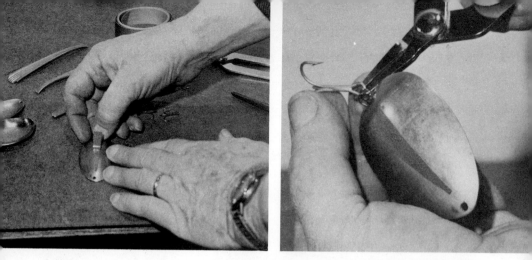

4. Hide worn spots or add flash with a bit of lure tape (above).

5. Use split rings to attach hooks, swivel (above right).

6. A home-made lure (right) — cost, less than 20¢ plus ten minutes work.

the way. The fact that manufacturers have batteries of presses that turn out 10,000 lure blades an hour from metal sheets doesn't mean that you need this kind of equipment to turn out uniformly good-looking, efficient blades. There are a lot of materials around that need little or no forming to produce spoon and spinner blades, and even starting from straight sheet metal you can turn out very good blades in dies you make yourself.

Get into the habit of looking at every metal object you run across in terms of its curves and contours, which, when cut into slices and filed a bit, will automatically produce a lure blade. Probably the most obvious example is the spoon. At junk or secondhand stores and garage sales, you can pick up spoons for a few pennies apiece. All you need do to convert them into wobbler-type and darter-type lures is to take off the handles, file the edges where you cut to remove saw or chisel marks, drill a couple of holes for split rings, attach hooks and a swivel to the rings, and you've got a ready-to-use lure.

A Lure from a Spoon Handle

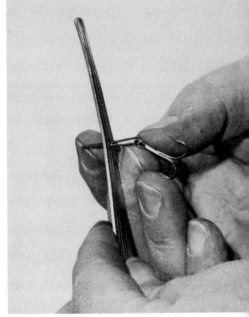

1. Flatten out the handle by hammering it on an anvil and drill a ⅛-inch hole in the center.

2. Bend a short length of lure wire into a tight U, put a hook on the wire, push the open ends through the hole in the spoon handle.

3. Bend the ends of the wire back around the handle edges and crimp them firmly.

4. Bend the handle into a tight U with the hooks at its bottom, then shape the handle into parallel curves; put a split ring in a hole drilled in one end for a line eye.

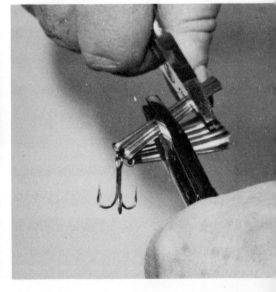

Don't discard the spoon handle; a bit of bending and drilling will turn it into a darter-type lure. Conversion of a spoon into a pair of lures with widely dissimilar actions is at best a ten- to fifteen-minute job, unless you've never touched tools before. And once you've acquired the habit of looking at metal objects with lures in mind, you'll see possibilities in all kinds of items that you can buy for next to nothing, perhaps that will be given to you free because they're not worth anything much to their owners.

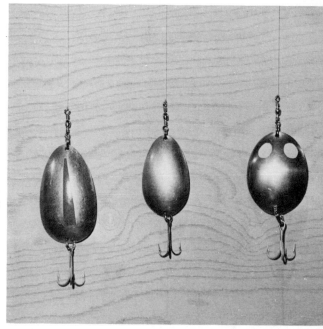

Three lures from three differently shaped spoons; each has its own action.

Look at the photos on page 28. The first shows a miscellaneous assortment of generally useless articles—useless, that is, to anybody but a lure maker. Their total cost was less than a dollar. Now, look at the second picture, which shows seventeen lures made from the otherwise worthless items in picture #1—and there was still a lot of raw lure material left in all the articles after these lures had been made, perhaps enough to produce twenty-five to thirty more lures. In the next chapter, we'll deal with the steps followed in these conversions.

Secondhand stores, junkyards, and garage sales have already been noted as a source of lure-making materials. To them add auto-wrecking yards, where you'll find discarded hubcaps and rearview mirror housings and an astonishing variety of other shiny metal objects that are potential lures. If you look closely at a hubcap, for example, you'll see that it consists of curves that closely match the contours of some of today's most popular and effective spoon and spinner blades. Battered hubcaps have minimal resale

Clockwise from top left, an electric-iron shell, an auto hood ornament, three simulated mother-of pearl plastic dress buckles, a chromed belt buckle, and the base of a stainless-steel gravy dish, picked up at garage sales. Total cost of everything, less than a dollar. All are good lure material.

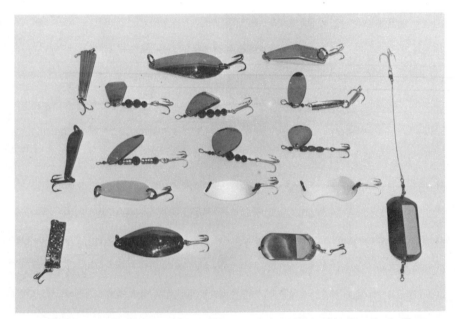

Vertically, at left, three lures, the top two made from spoon handles, the bottom one from half of one of the belt buckles shown in the preceding picture. A discarded rearview mirror shell provided the two lures at the top; those in the second row came from the iron shell; in the third row, a hubcap provided the blades, and the body of the spinning lure at right is made from a piece of the hood ornament seen in the preceding picture; the body of the lure at left in the third row is made from used caps for a muzzle-loading rifle, the blades of all three lures from a hubcap; the simulated mother-of-pearl plastic buckles shown in the preceding picture provided the three lures in the fourth row; the rearview mirror shell yielded the lure at left in the bottom row; the other two lures are made from scraps of stainless steel.

value, 2¢ to 4¢ a pound as scrap, and the dented hubcap you buy for 10¢ to 15¢ will produce from a dozen to twenty blades, even though you have to discard badly dented sections. We'll cover hubcaps in more detail in the next chapter.

Still another good source of raw materials is a local sheet-metal shop, a plumbing shop, an auto-body shop. Sheet-metal shops generally sweep the trimmings from objects they form into a scrap pile, which is sold to scrap-metal dealers by the pound at salvage prices. Most of these shops will sell to you at the same price, and a lot of them will give you scraps from time to time as long as you don't press them with often-repeated requests. Plumbing shops work with copper, which is a fine metal from which to fabricate blades for spoon- and spinner-type lures. Roofing contractors also work with copper in big sheets, and you might hit the sort of jackpot I did once, when I saw the all-copper roof of a church being repaired and for $2.00 got an assortment of scrap pieces that had enough material for over a thousand blades. But don't count on getting big bargains in copper; it's an expensive metal because it can be rerefined from scrap.

Auto-body shops usually have a lot of scrap from repair jobs, and a lot of lures can be produced from an old body panel or fender. The metal in most of today's cars, by the way, is thin enough to be worked easily. If you explore a body shop as a materials source, don't overlook its potential as a fountain of paints. The fountain flows in small quantities, but you don't need much paint in lure finishing. It's pretty general practice in body shops to mix just a bit more paint than is required for a job, and usually these small dribbles are discarded when the final touch-ups are completed. On a couple of occasions I've provided body shops with empty screw-top containers holding a half-pint or quarter-pint, into which they've poured various colors of enamel that would otherwise have gone down the drain. The cost? Nothing. They were happy to see the paint used instead of wasted.

WOOD BLOCKS

For making thick-bodied lures, or plugs, construction sites and cabinet shops have already been mentioned as sources of wood blocks big enough to use in making these lures. Occasionally, too, you'll hit a jackpot in a cabinet shop that will provide you with some pieces of close-grained hardwood suitable for use in making the dies from which metal spoon and spinner blades are formed. This, too, is a job that will be covered in a later chapter.

Every town, no matter how small, has usable lure-making materials going to waste. All you need to do in order to convert these to your use at little or no cost is to exercise a bit of thought and ingenuity in uncovering the sources. Incidentally, there's a certain protocol that I've worked out in tapping these potential sources. First of all, keep in mind that many of the fellows who work in these shops are fishermen themselves and are interested in what you're planning to do with the materials you're after. Don't be bashful about telling them, because in most cases they'll then show more energy in helping you find suitable materials than they would if you were looking for items to use for something that interested them less.

Next, always offer to buy the material you're after, even if it has little or no value to the shop. If the price placed on it is too high, you can always turn it down. But speaking from a certain amount of experience in this sort of scrap-scrounging, I've found that most of the time a price quoted will be fair and reasonable, and that you'll wind up with a lot more material than you pay for. In a lot of cases, you'll be given it free. Finally, always bring a lure or two as a gift to the shop's proprietor, should you discover that he's a fellow-fisherman, and also include a lure for any of the shop's employees who've gone out of their way to be helpful. Do this whether you get the material free or pay a nominal price for it. This isn't being especially generous or unselfish, it's more like insurance aimed at keeping a supply-line open.

No matter how successful you become at "managing" for lure materials, there will always be some items needed that you can't make yourself without spending more time than they're worth or investing in special tools that have limited use. Such small items as clevises and beads and split rings can't be successfully made by the amateur without a lot of time being spent in their fabrication. However, these items are so inexpensive that you don't tie up much cash in a stock big enough to take care of your needs, to give you variety in sizes, and to keep you from running out at a crucial moment. Hooks are among the items you can't successfully make, so buy them in the biggest quantities you feel you can afford to get the maximum savings.

You'll find, though, that the key to making lures costing only pennies apiece is the training you give yourself, not only in using tools, but in visualizing lure blades and bodies in items that most people think of as junk.

Now, let's go to work and turn out a few lures.

4

Thin-bodied Lures

THERE ARE A NUMBER of basic procedures common to the construction of all thin-bodied lures, whether you're assembling them from kits or components or building the lures from scratch. To save repetition, we'll cover all these common operations first, then in later pages they'll just be referred to as having already been explained and pictured. At that point, if your memory needs refreshing, all you need do is turn back a few pages.

You'll find that not all the procedures I recommend are totally orthodox or conventional. I don't feel called on to apologize for this, because nine times out of ten I started out following the standard procedure before finding a shortcut that was simpler and more practical. The old adage about having to know the rules before it's safe for you to break them doesn't always apply. Some craft procedures are actually the best way to do a job, but a lot of them are followed simply because they're traditional. As in the fable of the emperor's new clothes, it often takes someone with the unprejudiced mind of a child to point out what should be obvious to everybody.

Among the things you're not going to find in this or any other chapter are a lot of plans giving dimensions you'll be expected to follow meticulously. That sort of thing is fine in a factory, where standards are necessary in order for two or three different shifts of workers to produce thousands of identical, interchangeable items, but you're not setting up a factory production line, you're making a few lures for your own pleasure. If one out of three lures you make to the same pattern turns out to be a 32nd or a 64th of an inch bigger or smaller than the other two, the world's not going to come to an end.

When a dimension or angle is critical to the performance of a lure or one of its parts, this will be stated clearly, and it'll then be up to you to decide how closely you want to follow measurements. Who knows? If you ignore those measurements your lure might have a more effective action than if you'd followed them. It might also be a dud, but that's the risk an innovator takes.

Split-ring pliers have one wedge-shaped jaw tip that opens the ring, making it easy to slip the end into the hole of a lure or put it on a swivel eye.

When assembling thin-bodied lures from kits, the common job you'll do is to connect the components with one of three types of connectors: split rings, jump rings, or S-connectors. Split rings are easy to use if you've got split-ring pliers, a tool costing less than $1.00, which is made for this job and no other. It's one of the special-purpose tools that eases a niggling job. Just insert the straight tip of the pliers into the inside of the ring, close the pliers so that the angled, slanted tip bites into the space between the layers of the ring, and slip the opened portion of the ring into the hole in your lure. Add the hook eye or swivel, turn the ring until it encircles both lure and fitting, and that's it.

Most manufacturers use solid connectors, generally jump rings, because in assembly line work these are faster to fit. You can buy jump rings or make your own. To make them, you'll need heavy pliers, wire cutters, a length of #8 or #10 solid copper wire — tinned if you want shiny rings — and a couple of feet of ³⁄₈-inch or ½-inch dowel. You can use the wire salvaged by stripping insulation from standard electrical house wiring of the correct gauge and straightening it out.

Set the dowel in a vise, upright. Holding one end of the wire with pliers, wrap the wire around the dowel in a tight spiral. Slip the wire off the dowel and cut through at roughly the same place on each turn. Squeeze the rings that result to cure any irregularities and pull them together. If you want to be meticulous, square off the slanted cut ends with a file. A foot of wire on a ³⁄₈-inch diameter dowel produces about ten to a dozen rings. To use them, slip the eye of the hook or swivel and the eye of the lure blade into the opening and gently squeeze the ring closed. A little practice will teach you the point at which to squeeze in order to produce a perfectly round ring when its ends meet. These rings won't pull apart under the pressure of any freshwater fish you're likely to hook; your line will break before the ring pulls open. If you're worried about this, or if you're making rings to be used in saltwater fishing, solder the joint after the lure's completed.

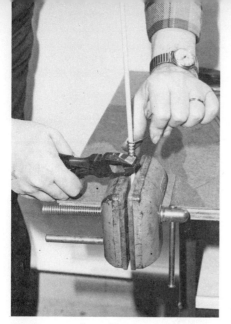

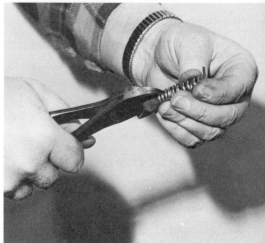

The first step in making jump rings is to wrap a foot or so of #8 or #10 copper wire around a dowel chucked in a vise.

Slide the spiral of wire off the dowel and clip up it, cutting each turn; cut in a reasonably straight line.

S-connectors are a type of double jump ring, one I've never been able to figure out how to make quickly and easily. Like split rings and a few other lure components, they're better made with factory facilities. You can get along very well without S-connectors, as they perform the same functions as split or round jump rings; if you feel you need them or want to use them, they're not expensive to buy.

Forming loops or eyes in spinner wire is a job you'll be doing as often as you'll fit split rings or jump rings, especially if you make a lot of spinners or lures of the Abu-Mepps type, or a lot of trolling rigs. Let me start with a word of advice based on experience. Do use regular spinner wire instead of piano wire. Spinner wire is just as tough, but a lot easier to work with. Piano wire is very brittle and stiff and has a nasty habit of breaking when pulled into a tight wrap.

Use your homemade jump rings just as you would those made in a factory: open them to take a hook and pass through the hook eye of a lure blade, squeeze with pliers to close.

Forming an Eye on a Jig

1. Bring the ends of a length of wire around one of the arms; allow 1½ to 2 inches of working material on the end in which the eye will be made.

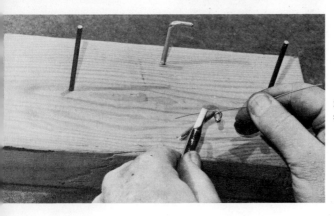

2. Make the loop as tight as possible; use pliers to tighten it.

3. Holding the short end in the pliers, make as tight a wrap as possible around the long end of the wire.

4. Make two more tight wraps. Then, using the very tip of a pair of cutters, trim off the excess.

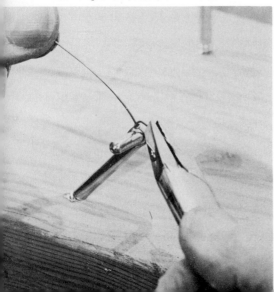

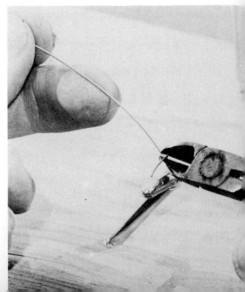

Spinner wire is available in several gauges or diameters, ranging from .020 (20 thousandths of an inch) to .035. The smaller the diameter, the easier the wire is to work, but lures made on spinner-wire shafts smaller than .024 tend to be flimsy, and when you get into wire gauges above .029 the wire's hard to work. You might start out by using .024 wire until you get the feel of it, then move up to a larger gauge if you feel that the .024 wire is too delicate.

Of course, if you want to go the easy way, you can buy ready-formed spinner shafts with both open and closed eyes. These shafts are available in lengths from 3 to 8 inches, but even if you use them you are still going to have to form the final eye, and once you've gotten the knack of forming eyes it's as easy to form two as it is one.

FORMING EYE LOOPS

There are two options available in making eye loops. One is to work on a jig, the other is to work freehand with two pairs of pliers. The jig pictured earlier is very simple to make and use, and sometimes answers your wish for that third hand you feel you need when forming eyes freehand with pliers. It's especially handy when you're forming eyes that enclose a hook or swivel.

When using the jig, make your first bend around the forming arm, bringing the wire completely around the end of the arm. Then, with the jaws of your pliers under the standing end of the wire—the end that will become your spinner shaft—get a firm grip on the short end of the wire and pull it in a quick, firm movement to wrap around the standing end. Use the standing end of the wire as a fulcrum for the jaws of your pliers. Repeat this process three times; three wraps of leader wire are enough to make a firm eye that won't pull out. Clip off the excess wire with cutters and straighten the shaft in relation to the eye as necessary.

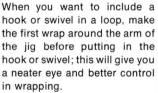

When you want to include a hook or swivel in a loop, make the first wrap around the arm of the jig before putting in the hook or swivel; this will give you a neater eye and better control in wrapping.

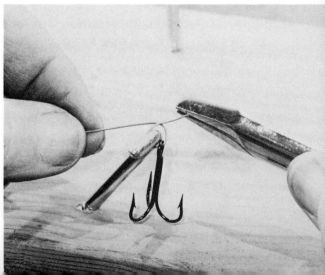

This sounds easier than it is in actual practice, but practice is the key. After you've formed a few spinners it'll take you about forty-five seconds to make a perfect eye.

When forming an eye that encloses a hook or swivel, make the first wrap around the forming arm before slipping in the hook eye, then proceed with your tight wraps of the short wire-end around the standing portion. You may have a hump in your eye where the hook or swivel has bound against the forming arm, but this can easily be taken out by squeezing it between the jaws of your roundnose pliers.

Forming an eye freehand is basically the same process as forming it on a jig; the jaws of your roundnose pliers simply take the place of the arm, and you form the eye around one side of the jaws. You'll work out your own angles of work after you've done a bit of experimenting, but I find it easier to hold the roundnose pliers upright in my left hand and work with the bending pliers in my right. The procedure is about the same. Begin by making a 180-degree wrap around one jaw of the pliers holding the wire. Then, grasp the short end of the wire firmly with the second pliers and twist the short end tightly around the standing end. Remember to use the standing end of the wire as a fulcrum against which your plier jaws lever, and you won't have any trouble making nice, tight twists. You will have one extra step in the job when forming eye loops on pliers: the circumference of the loop will have taken on the contour of the plier jaws; it'll be a bit flat on one side. Squeeze it into a circle with the jaws of the pliers.

One of the eyes in the final picture of the loop-making sequence was formed on a jig, and one on pliers. The wraps in one were purposely spaced out to show the actual formation of the three turns required for a breakproof eye. However, you might have trouble determining which of the eyes was made on the jig, and which on the pliers. Forming on pliers, by the way, has one advantage over forming on a jig: you can take advantage of the taper in the roundnose pliers to form eyes of several different sizes, something you can't do on a jig unless you provide forming arms of different diameters.

Those extra arms on the jig, by the way, are for use in spacing shaft lengths uniformly. After the shaft has been fitted with blades and whatever else goes on it, slip the eye over a vertical arm and form the second eye on the horizontal arm—or vice versa, if you find it easier to work that way. Shafts formed in this manner will be of uniform length.

Forming eye loops is about the most complicated job you'll encounter when making thin-bodied lures, and the ease with which you learn to perform this operation is going to have an effect on the pleasure you'll get from lure making. While you practice this procedure until you can do it quickly and without worrying how your eye's going to come out, the spinner wire that you use up won't be wasted material. Practice a lot and charge the few inches of wire used to experience.

Forming a Loop with Pliers

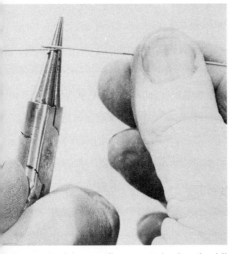

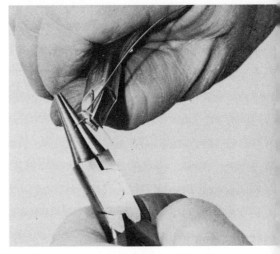

1. Make your first wrap by hand while holding the wire firmly in the round tapered jaws. When your wrap is finished, the long and short ends of the wire should be in a straight line across the outside of the pliers' nose.

2. Keep the lever-and-fulcrum idea in mind as you work, keep the nose of the wrapping pliers as close as possible to the leader pliers and use the long end of the wire to give your pliers leverage as you turn them. The tapered-nose pliers are held still during the operation.

3. Three tight turns are enough to make a loop that will hold against any pressure it will get from a fish.

4. After trimming excess wire from your cutters, straighten up the loop where it's been flattened by the jaws of the tapered-nose leader pliers.

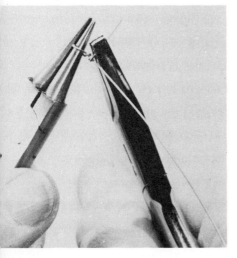

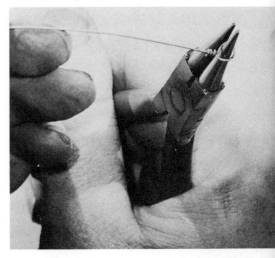

FORMING BLADES

Now we come to the second most complicated job of lure fabricating, the craft or art of forming blades. You've already seen how the bowl of a spoon can be converted into a lure with very little effort, but I've a hunch that while you were digesting the few paragraphs and pictures devoted to that, you were skeptically thinking: "That's all very well, but what happens if I want something besides a spoon-shaped blade?" Relax, it's not all that difficult.

Let's begin with the dies. Most metals that you'll want to use for lure blades can be worked in hardwood dies. After you've made perhaps fifty to seventy-five blades in a wooden die, it'll have to be reworked or a new one made. The working life of a wooden die depends on the quality and kind of wood used in making it. If you want long-lasting dies, hardrock maple is the wood to use. I buy shotgun forearm blanks in the lowest available grade, since I'm not looking for fancy graining, but tough wood. These blanks cost from $1.50 to $3.00 in maple, from $1.75 to $4.00 in myrtle wood, and from $1.25 to $2.50 in cherry wood. Any of these woods makes a die that will last a long time, and the typical blank is big enough to accommodate six or eight dies, using both sides of the wood. There's a less ex-

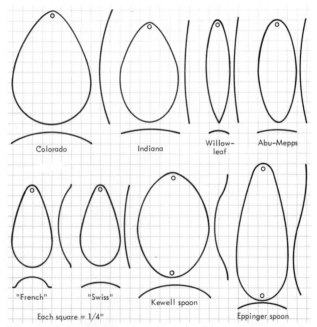

Colorado   Indiana   Willow-leaf   Abu–Mepps

"French"   "Swiss"   Kewell spoon   Eppinger spoon

Each square = 1/4"

These scaled outlines and profiles of spinner contours can be enlarged or reduced to suit your needs; use them as described in the text to help you make dies or to make the actual blades.

Begin with a burr for fast-cutting action, and rough out the die cavity. Score a centerline with the burr and work along it first to one side, then to the other. Don't try to take off too much wood at one pass, make many shallow passes instead.

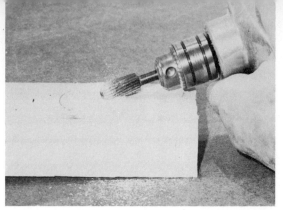

When the cavity's been roughened out, switch to the stones; use the shapes best suited for the size and type of die you're making. Use light pressure and keep the stone moving. Check often with your template for depth and contour. The stones give you a smoother finish than you can get using sandpaper. When cavity and template match, the die is finished.

pensive wood stocked by many lumber dealers, Pyrana Pine, which is a bit softer than maple, but a lot better than oak or walnut.

Start your die making by tracing the outline of the blade shape you're going to make. To help you, there are patterns of various kinds of blades illustrated; use these to make templates that give you not only the shapes of the blades, but their curvature. Or, you can simply trace the blade you want to reproduce directly on the blank from which you'll form your die.

Use rotary burrs and stones in your electric drill to rout out the inner curves you're after. Make a few passes first with the coarse-cutting burrs, then switch to the stone to finish up the job and give your die a smooth surface. Even in hardwoods, making a die this way is a matter of minutes. You could use metals for dies and get a much longer life from them, but you'd also spend a lot more time forming the cavity.

Making a die in this manner is pretty much a matter of cut-and-try. Don't work too fast, or you'll have fluted ridges in the cavity. Take it easy, burr out a bit and gauge the depth and contour of the forming cavity with your template, then burr out some more until you're ready to finish off with the stones.

Your die is ready for use immediately. To form a blade in it, first cut a square or rectangle about ½ inch larger in all dimensions than the size of the blade you'll be making. Mark the ends and sides at the point where the die is longest and widest, then with tinsnips cut small slits all around the metal blank. This is to keep wrinkles from forming as the metal is drawn into the die.

Unless your blank is of very hard, thick metal, don't work on it with a hammer. Use planishing sticks—short lengths of hardwood dowel filed and sanded into convex contours on one end. Form one into an oval shape, the other into a shallow round curve.

Now, center the metal blank over the die and with the round-end planishing stick tap lightly along its entire length. Don't try to hit the bottom of the die the first time around. Strike the stick with gentle taps until you've bottomed out, then work from the center to the sides, alternating left and right of the center, to establish the blade's contours.

At this point your metal blank is going to begin buckling and wrinkling up. Take it out of the die and tap it with the planishing tool on the anvil to remove any wrinkles that extend into the metal of the blade's final shape. Do this with light, repeated taps of the hammer rather than giant-strong licks.

Return the blank to the die, making sure it's positioned properly, and work again from the centerline to the edges until the blade is formed. Use the oval stick to work close to the edges and into the narrow ends of the metal. Go back to the anvil to take out any new wrinkles that form. When your blank has bottomed out on all parts of the die, trim off the excess metal, leaving a rim of about ⅛ to 1/16 inch all around the blade.

Go back to the die, position the trimmed blade in it, and take out as many bumps as possible by tapping with the hammer and pressing down on the planishing tool with all your strength while working it back and forth over the blade. You'll be able to smooth out most uneven spots this way, but for the final shaping you'll have to go to the jeweler's bag.

This leather sand-filled bag is one of your handiest accessories in shaping a lure blade. To use it in removing small dents and bumps, pound a cavity in it with your fist, lay the blade on the bag's surface and tap gently with planishing tool and hammer until the dent is gone. Remember, gently, gently does it on the tapping.

Finally, when all the dents and wrinkles are smoothed away, give the blade its final contour trimming and smooth its edges with a fine-cut file, finishing off with crocus cloth. You can then buff the blade, use metal polish on it, paint it or cover it with lure tape to give it the finishing touch.

When forming small blades, it's easier and faster to use a set of dies, male and female. In fact, blades of a fairly respectable size can be formed this way, though there's a relationship between the size of the blade and depth of draw in the die that limits you in forming very big blades with the male-female die set. Shallow draws can be made in fairly large blanks, but a

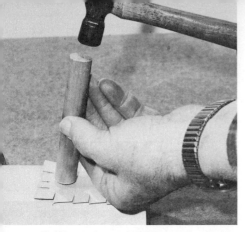

1. Place the prepared blank over die. Tap the stick lightly, moving it a fraction of an inch between each tap. Go over the entire die area this way until your blank bottoms out against the die.

2. When wrinkles begin to form—and they will—move the blank to the anvil and iron them out with the round planishing stick. Again, gentle, repeated tapping does the job. When the wrinkle's out, put the blank back in the die and go on working; be sure it's properly centered.

Forming a Spinner Blade

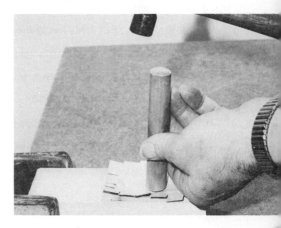

3. When your blank is touching bottom all around the die, establish the outer lines by going around the edges of the die's cavity with the oval planishing stick. Don't let the blank shift while you're doing this or you'll have an off-center blade.

4. After rough-trimming the blank, put it back in the die and use the planishing sticks to smooth the blank as much as possible. If the metal used is soft and thin enough, this is more effective than using a hammer on the sticks, which you'll have to do with heavy metals.

5. All jeweler's bags are different, and you'll just have to learn the feel of the one you're using to know how much force to use in your hammer-taps during the final forming, which is chiefly removing dents.

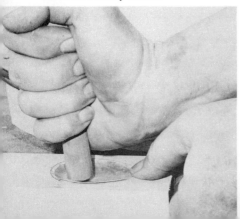

When using a die set you can use heavier hammer blows. The blanks for the blades are made just as you'd make them for an open die.

width of 1¼" to 1½" is about the limit on outside dimensions if the draw is deep, as for a spoon.

Make your die set by forming the female half in a wood block, then carve the male die in the grain-end of a piece of wood. Use carbon paper to test for a good fit between male and female; press the male die into the cavity with a slip of carbon paper between the two dies to find high or low spots in either one.

Because the male die inhibits the metal blank from wrinkling, you can use much more forceful blows with your hammer when forming the blades. Just be sure that the male die is held vertically at a 90-degree angle to the female, or you'll produce lopsided blades. Trim and planish the blades as already detailed, and finish off by filing and smoothing the edges of the blades.

You can also improvise dies from such steel forms as hammerheads and work metal blanks on them freehand, using a hard rubber or leather mallet to keep from damaging the metal with sharp dents. The only trick to producing blades this way is that, since you'll be working entirely by eye, you must stop frequently to gauge contours and curvature. Often, of course, errors of this kind can be corrected by judicious trimming away of lopsides; you'll wind up with a smaller blade than you'd planned on by doing this, but you can always start over and make a bigger one.

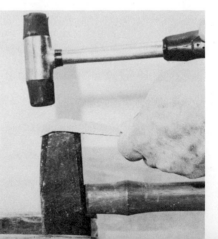

Open dies, male or female, can be improvised from a lot of everyday tools, such as hammers. Use a rubber or hide mallet to reduce damage to the surface of the metal, but be prepared to do a lot of buffing.

42

Working freehand on the jeweler's bag is another possibility you should explore. Often when you want a very shallow curve in a blade, you can save the time and trouble of making a die by tapping out the blade freehand, using the bag as an anvil. If you work in this style, cut the blade to its approximate contour before you begin to shape it, leaving enough edge-space to allow for a final trimming that will correct any errors you might have made during your freehand forming. And always remember when working on the jeweler's bag that gentle, repeated tapping, moving the planishing tool a fraction of an inch between taps, is the way to work — not heavy, pounding blows.

There are, of course, practical limits to the depth of blade contours you can produce with wooden dies. There are also practical limits to the thickness of the metals you can work in them, and you will find that some kinds of metal work more easily than do others.

SHEET METALS

If you're new to sheet metals, here are some tips. Copper is the easiest of all sheet metals to work — if you anneal it at intervals as you draw your spinner or spoon blades into the die. Copper tends to get hard and brittle when worked; annealing restores its ductility. It's no great task to anneal; just hold the work in pliers and put it in the middle of a blowtorch or LP gas torch until it turns color, then remove it, let the metal cool, and go on working it. You can draw deeper, stronger blades — for spoons and wobblers, for instance — more easily from copper than from any other metal.

Black sheet iron is next in line for ease of working, but it cannot be annealed to restore ductility lost as it is being shaped. Stainless steel of the #400 type is about on a par with black sheet iron and has the advantage of being much easier to finish. However, avoid the #300 type of stainless steel, for it's hard, brittle, and very difficult to work. Sheet tin — actually, tin plate — is easy to work, but its surface mars very easily. Aluminum works easily but is not heavy enough for spoon blades; it makes good Abu-Mepps-type spinner blades, however, and is easy to buff to a high shine. Brass is a hard metal to work with, though it's delightful to finish and makes very good blades with an excellent weight-to-size factor. Galvanized sheet metal is relatively brittle and very troublesome to finish, unless lure tape is used as the finishing medium.

These are the kinds of metals you'll be most likely to encounter. I'm ignoring the precious metals, gold and silver, though once upon a river I met a pair of ultrarich anglers, one of whom had a set of sterling silver spinners with his name engraved on them, while the other owned a pair of 14-karat gold spinners set with tiny rubies. I watched the pair fishing for a while, and their spinners didn't seem to be any more attractive to the fish than did mine of baser metals. However, both gold and silver are easy metals to work with, if you feel rich enough to try them.

Getting back to earth, all sheet metal is gauged in numbers, such as 20-gauge, 24-gauge, and so on, the diminishing numbers in the sequence representing an increase in thickness. For all practical purposes in lure making, we can ignore all but a few thicknesses. Ferrous sheet metal, such as tin plate and black sheet iron, can be worked readily in 28-, 26-, and 24-gauge; respectively, these numbers represent sheet thicknesses of .019, .022, and .024 inches. If you go to a sheet metal thinner than 28-gauge, it's going to make too flimsy a blade; if you go to sheet iron heavier than 24-gauge, it's going to be too hard to work. In copper, though, you can readily work 22- and 20-gauge sheet, and in aluminum you can go as low as 18-gauge if your draw is not too deep.

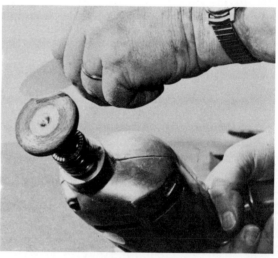

Dress ornaments of plastic are easy to form by grinding; use a wheel in an arbor on a hand drill if you don't own a bench grinder. Most plastics are too light and flimsy for lures, but dense plastics between ¹/₁₆ and ¹/₈ inch thick make good, light spinning lures.

Now, let's look at some of the metals you'll run into when you start making lure blades of odd objects salvaged from garage sales, auto-wrecking yards, and similar sources. For a lot of these, you'll have no precise frame of reference, so we're going to have to fall back on generalities. Perhaps the best way to handle this matter is to go back to the salvaged items pictured earlier and the lures made from them, and hit the high spots of the processes by which plastic dress ornaments, a belt buckle, the shell of an electric iron, and the base of a broken lamp became lures.

Of the group, the plastic simulated mother of pearl dress ornaments were easiest to convert. Turning them into spoon-type wobbling lures was just a matter of prying off the thin brass buckles with which they were decorated and grinding them to shape on a coarse stone chucked in an electric drill. Since the material was too thick to allow use of split rings, jump rings were used to attach hooks and swivels. The job of turning the three buckles into lures took about twenty minutes.

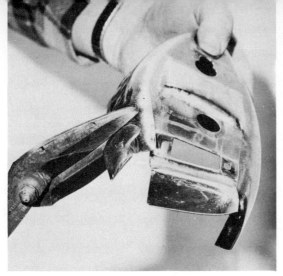

Once the way to attack it with tinsnips was solved, the iron shell was easy to work and yielded eighteen lure blades with a bonus of the bench anvil, shown earlier, from the iron.

In order to use tinsnips in cutting blanks from the iron shell, it was necessary to cut pieces from each corner of the back part. The snips were then used to cut the shell into rectangular strips, which already had a nice curve in them. After the curvature had been deepened a bit in a die, the rectangles were snipped down into spinner-shaped pieces and filed to size. The iron shell yielded fifteen blades, and the top part was still left to be cut up; it provided three blades.

Working the lamp base was a bit harder; it proved to be of one of the #400 stainless steels and had to be sawed by hand with a tungsten carbide blade in the hacksaw. It was cut into triangular strips about 1 inch wide at the base, and from it came an even dozen blades. The hood ornament, sawed into short lengths, provided the bodies for seventeen Abu-Mepps-type spinning lures, and the belt buckle made three darter lures similar to the SuperDuper.

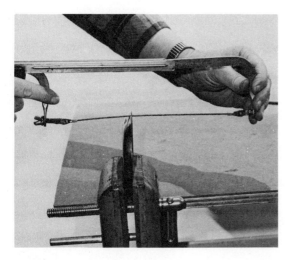

Hardest to work was the gravy-boat base; a tungsten carbide hacksaw blade was needed to cut blanks from it. The satin-finished metal burnished down into good blades, though.

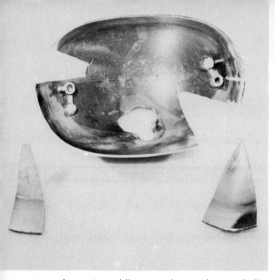

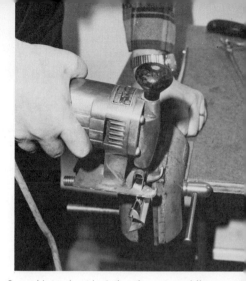

An automobile rearview mirror shell shows how blanks can be cut to take advantage of a junk object's natural curves and contours.

Sawed into short lengths, the automobile hood ornament provided twenty-three spinning-lure bodies.

There are in the picture of the lures a couple that were made from the shell of an automobile's outside rearview mirror; the mirror with two blanks sawed from it is shown in an accompanying picture. The mirror body, like so many modern ornamental automotive details, was cast from an alloy of zinc, tin, copper, and antimony, which can be worked quite easily with saw and file, even though they are fairly thick. If you work much with scrounged auto trim parts in making lures, you'll be encountering this alloy quite often, and if you use a saber or jig saw to cut it into blanks, be sure to wax the saw blade before cutting to prevent the metal melting and clogging the teeth. Because of its thickness and brittle nature, you won't be able to work pieces of this metal in dies or on the jeweler's bag; your blades must be sawed and filed or ground into shape utilizing the original contours of the casting.

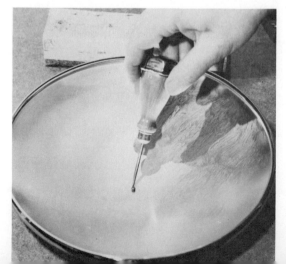

To find the center of a domed hubcap that has no insignia mark to help you, drop a BB or shotgun pellet into the cap.

Hubcaps are made from a similar alloy, though they are thinner and much more ductile. Because salvaged hubcaps are an especially good source of lure blanks, let's go into some detail on how to handle them to get the greatest number of blanks possible. For photographic purposes, the pictures illustrating the hubcap-to-lures conversion were made using a new hubcap, which cost $1.60 in its factory wrappings. If you're working with a used cap, you'll of course have to plan your cuts to avoid any dents or battered spots.

Before cutting, the first job is to determine the center of the hubcap so that you can calculate its circumference easily and plan your cuts. The easiest way to find the apex of an unmarked dome is to drop a BB shot or some other kind of small round pellet into the cap while it's upended on a

If you want blade blanks of equal size, cut a tab of cardboard the width of the widest dimension into which the circumference can be divided equally and use it as a jig to mark off equal segments.

level surface. The BB will roll to the center, which is then marked with a punch and a hole drilled in it. Putting a rule across the edges, with the rule passing over the hole, gives you the diameter, which is multiplied by our old friend, pi—3.1416, in case you've forgotten—to get the circumference.

Next, divide the circumference by the width of the blades you plan to make from the hubcap's metal. For the sake of argument, let's say the cap in the picture is going to be turned into #5 Colorado spinner blades, which are 1⅜ inches wide. This means cutting the hubcap into triangles a bit more than 1½ inches wide at their base. The upper parts of these pieces won't be wasted, of course, but used for smaller blades. We've already determined that the hubcap is 32.9 inches in circumference—33 inches for all practical purposes—so dividing our blade blank width into that gives us a yield of twenty-one strips. Cut a piece of cardboard into a 1⅝-inch square, and use it as a template to mark off the segments at the hubcap's rim.

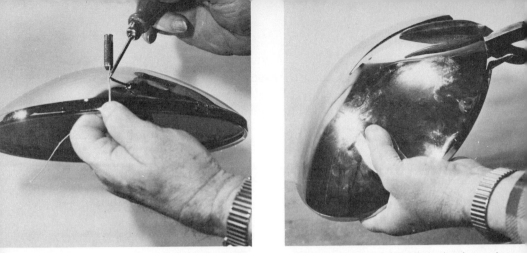

Drop a nail or punch into the hole drilled in the cap's top center, stretch a cord tightly to the rim marks and score along the cord to mark your cut-lines. Cut the metal with snips or aviation shears.

Now, put a nail or your punch in the hole drilled at the top of the hubcap, tie a loop in the end of a piece of string, and drop the loop over the nail or punch. Stretched tight from that point to the rim, the string will give you a line along which to mark your cutting lines.

What you do next depends on the method you intend to use to cut the cap. If you're going to use a saw, leave the rim intact for stability. If you're going to use snips or a nibbling tool, the rim must come off, so snip out just above it and use pliers to bend back the cut part so that your snips will have working room. If you're cutting with a power saw, be sure to put strips of masking tape along each side of the cutting line so that the saw's soleplate won't scratch the cap's surface. A jig saw is the ideal tool, but if you're very familiar with power saws you'll know that a circular saw can be used to cut thin metals of this type by putting in an old blade with the teeth reversed. Cut along the lines from rim to center, and you wind up with material for forty-two lure blades, half of them large, half small. If the smaller blades are small enough, you might get another twenty-one willow-leaf-type blades from the thin upper sections of the blanks.

Mark the bottom sections for your spinner blanks, which are snipped out roughly, trimmed, and filed to their final shape. Incidentally, these triangular strips also make ideal blanks for the big triangular blades of the Ford Fender trolling rig.

Hubcaps bought from wrecking yards usually cost you the scrap price of the metal, which at the time this is written is 5¢ to 6¢ a pound. This means that you'll be paying 20¢ to 25¢ for a hubcap that even if a bit dented and battered will yield around forty lure blades for a cost of about ½¢ per blade, as compared with the current going price of 12¢ to 15¢ per factory-made blade. At this rate, you can afford to discard the dented areas of a hubcap and still be ahead.

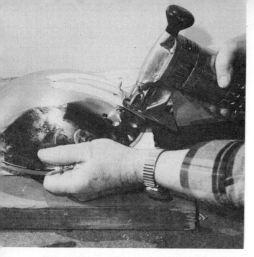

If a power saw is used, put masking tape along the cut-lines to avoid scratching the metal's finish with the soleplate.

Each triangular blank cut from the half-moon-type hubcap will yield three spinner blades in decreasingly smaller sizes.

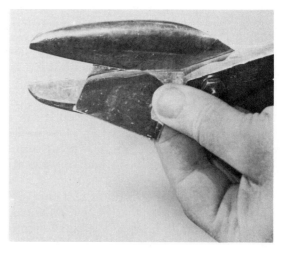

Snip carefully, taking off small pieces, when rough-trimming to preserve the metal's natural curves. The spinner blades from most hubcaps have a natural concave shape that makes them spin rather slowly; if you want a fast spinner, deepen the blanks on the jeweler's bag or in a die.

After trimming, filing, and finish-polishing, you'll need only to drill a clevis hole to have a completed blade.

With very little handwork, the triangular pieces make almost perfectly shaped blades for the popular Ford Fender troll.

ASSEMBLING LURES

Now, let's look at the way lures are assembled. Actually, you have only two basic types of assembly for the most popular thin-bodied lures, the straight spinner and the bodied or Abu-Mepps-type spinner. Their assembly is very similar, but the differences are nonetheless important.

A basic spinner can be as simple as a blade on a shaft, but most spinners incorporate some kind of attractor in their make-up. It's usually a few red or orange beads, sometimes a bucktail-covered hook, sometimes both beads and bucktail.

Start out with an eyed shaft about 3 inches long. Put on a small to medium-sized bead, then assemble the clevis and spinner and slide them on the shaft. Remember, the outer curve of the spinner blade must *always* face the line eye or the spinner won't spin. You also need the front bead to act as a bearing and keep the clevis from jamming in the bottom of the eye. Thread on three or four more beads—traditionally, they're graduated in size from large to small—and form the back eye around the hook. That's the Colorado spinner, one of the most popular thin-bodied lures, and one that has enjoyed top rank in popularity for almost a century.

There's very little difference in the assembly of a straight spinner and the so-called French or Swiss or Abu-Mepps-type lure. The chief difference is the blade shape, which is usually thin and shallow-curved. Such blades don't take off as readily as the more deeply curved Colorado or Indiana blades, so you need a bearing on either side of the clevis to make sure the delicate blade will keep spinning. These bearings are brass balls of infinitesimal size, called "unies" for some mysterious reason. Be sure you have one on each side of the clevis when you assemble your lures. The bodies of these spinners can be beads, torpedo- or cigar- or bullet-shaped lead castings, brass rings, copper tubing, ceramic cylinders—just about anything you choose to use, decorated any way that you wish. But the assembly is almost identical with that of a straight spinner: on an eyed shaft 3½ to 4 inches long, thread a unie, a clevis-blade assembly, another unie, the body, then form the rear eye with a hook inside.

Generally speaking, when you put together any spinner assembly, you're going to need a bead of some sort on either side of the tiny clevis to insure that the latter doesn't jam on a tip of wire at the eye loop. Trolling lures are generally put together with single beads fore and aft of each blade. The shafts on which the blades are strung should be roughly as long as the blade on the shaft ahead, so that the blades won't engage in submarine warfare. There are few standards for trolling rigs; usually the size and number of blades are geared to lake depth and average fish size. One thing to keep in mind is that a few trolling rigs use blades that rotate in opposite directions, and you should be careful to get the blades placed properly so that the troll will have the desired action.

One more thing to bear in mind, if you're using open-eyed spinner shafts: on these shafts, the assembly is the reverse of that used when put-

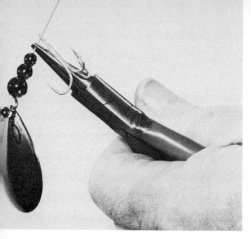

A typical Colorado spinner assembly: small front bead bearing, the blade on its clevis — it won't spin without the clevis — and three or four beads between blade and hook. This one will be complete as soon as the hook eye is formed.

Spinning lures of the Abu-Mepps type are put together much like the Colorado. One difference is the use of tiny metal beads on each side of the clevis; these are called "unies," I know not why.

The body of this kind of spinning lure can be beads, tubular lead or brass castings, almost anything. In one of the pictures there's a lure of this kind I made from used muzzle-loader caps.

Assemble trolling lures by stringing several spinner blades on shafts, using beads on both sides of the clevises for bearings. Form the shafts with linked loops of the shaft wire, or string them together with split rings or jump rings.

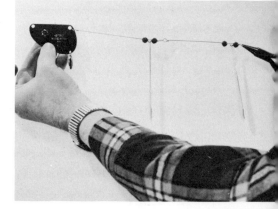

ting a lure on a closed-eye shaft. You start out with the hook and use the beads or body to close the eye by slipping them over the open end of the loop as well as the shaft. And you wind up with your blade, ahead of which you'll form the line eye as already detailed.

FINISHING BLADES

Now let's get into the matter of finishes for your lure blades and, if and when necessary, bodies. Blades are your chief concern, and you'll spend a lot more time gussying them up than you will on trying to add color to the body, which is either secondary or nonexistent in the kind of lure we're now working with.

One of the reasons for using such objects as electric iron shells, rearview mirror frames, hubcaps, and so on is because they are preplated, finished with tough plating that will withstand a moderate amount of rough treatment while you're making a lure blade from them. Usually, if you're reasonably careful, your blade will need only a bit of buffing with a nonscratchy cleaning-buffing compound to shine like the sun itself. Ideally, you won't have anything more than this to do if you start out with a preplated metal.

Stainless steel lure blades need fairly extensive buffing with a medium-coarse, then a fine, buffing compound. You can do this by hand using a coarse cloth, or you can fit a small buffing wheel into an arbor that can be chucked into your drill. If you make blades of aluminum, a fine buffing compound will get them to shine brightly.

Copper lures can be cleaned with household cleaners; there is a regular formula for copper that is used with plain tap water. It's very easy to use.

If you've used a dull-surfaced metal for your lure blades, you have several options. On black sheet iron there are a couple of liquid finishes designed to simulate chrome. Both of them are messy to use and require that the blade be almost surgically clean before being dipped or brushed; the blade must then be baked and buffed. You'll be time and money ahead if you pass up these finishes, because you won't be satisfied with them if you're at all particular, and because there are quicker, better ways of doing the job.

Paint is one way. There are tough new acrylic- and epoxy-based enamels that will cling well to a lure blade and that are virtually scratchproof and chip-proof. The epoxy paints need a special epoxy undercoating, but if you're dipping your blades, which is the fast and economical way to paint them, that's a small problem. If you want two-tone effects, masking tape will cover the portion of the blade that must be left bare for the contrasting color. If you're using a light and a dark color, dip the light color first, mask off the area you don't want the dark color to cover — waiting, of course, for the first coat to dry bone-hard — and then put on the dark coat.

You can spray lures with automotive finishes that most parts supply houses carry in a rainbow of hues; these finishes today are generally acrylic-

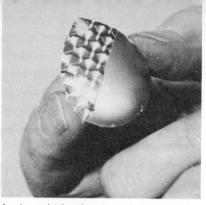

Peel off the backing from the tape and press it on the blade, then trim as shown. The tape's tough, so use a sharp knife.

Apply and trim the second piece of tape with its contrasting finish and tone. And the desired effect is complete.

based and very tough. And don't forget the body shop when planning your painting; this was mentioned earlier as a source of supply for small quantities of a variety of colors. Usually, you'll get enough to dip a lure or two in. (See the next chapter for further suggestions on painting lures.)

Tapes are gaining great popularity in the field of lure decorating. In the appendix you'll find sources for these tapes, if you can't find them locally. They are the tapes that airlines use to put numbers on jet planes, and that racing-car drivers use to put stripes, numbers, and other decor on their cars, so you know they'll stand up.

These new tapes are very easy to use and highly flexible; you can even apply them to curved forms like spoons and spinners without a great deal of difficulty. To cover a spinner blade just cut a square of the tape a bit bigger than the blade, peel off the backing, and press down firmly. On blades with pronounced curvature the tape will probably form a crease or

On a deeply drawn blade the tape may pucker. To cure this, first press the tape out from the center before the backing adhesive sets firmly to consolidate a number of small wrinkles into a single big one or two, then slice down the center of the wrinkle or wrinkles.

Lift one side of the cut; it won't be attached firmly to the blade yet, and the tip of your knife will pick it up. Press the other side down firmly. let the flap your knife holds settle down on top, overlapping, and press it into place.

wrinkle toward the outer rim of the blade; remove this by slicing down the center of the pucker with the tip of a sharp knife or razor blade, lift the tape on one side of the cut, press on the lower tape, bring the section you've lifted over the triangle of tape below it, which is now stuck on the lure blade, and press again. This leaves a seam in your finish, but it won't be noticed by a fish.

As a final precaution, whether you finish your lure blades *au naturel,* or with paint, or with tape, give them a final dipping in a clear acrylic or polyurethane varnish. The full colors or shine of the lures will still come through, but your lures will be sealed against tarnishing and discoloring, and protected against the scratches they might otherwise pick up from being scraped over rocks when you're fishing them deeply.

A final word on the subject of this type of lure making. Don't be afraid to experiment with unconventional shapes in spoon and spinner blades. Factories have a problem in this respect. They've learned that most fishermen are pretty conventional when it comes to buying lures, and they therefore look for familiar shapes and patterns. Even though all lure manufacturers do experimental and pilot work in developing new lures, it's very costly for them to tool up a production line for the introduction of a lure with an unconventional shape.

On the other hand, it costs you practically nothing to try out a new form in a lure blade. There's no law that compels you to follow custom or tradition in constructing spinner blades or in putting new lures together. Give your imagination free play. Try new shapes in blades, new combinations of colors, new patterns of assembly. You just might hit on some combination that nobody's yet tried, one that will produce strikes beyond any fisherman's wildest dreams.

5

Thick-bodied Lures

ALTHOUGH THE THICK-BODIED lure family has proliferated wildly since Jim Heddon first started whittling on cedar plugs, the shape of these lures has undergone alteration and modification rather than basic change. Even the very newest model plugs are still elongated cylinders designed to resemble a small fish. Sometimes the bodies are flattened, elongated, curved, or twisted, and there have been a lot of changes in their finish, but these changes have been evolutionary, not revolutionary. Plugs have undergone refinements resulting from a better understanding of the dynamics of underwater motion, from new materials and methods of fabrication, and from the improvements in tackle that have reduced plugs in size and bulk.

You have the same options in making thick-bodied lures that are open to you in making those of the thin-bodied family. You can buy kits that typically contain several bodies, either unfinished or painted, along with screw eyes for hooks and line, perhaps washers to go between hook eyes and bodies, nose scoops, and whatever else is needed to produce complete plugs when all the pieces are put in their proper places. Or, you can buy components separately, bodies and the necessary hardware, which gives you a little bit more leeway but is still essentially an assembly job. This is the easiest way to go, and it does save you a substantial amount of money in comparison to the cost of ready-made lures.

Your creativity and imagination will have more scope, and your savings will be greater, if you go the third route, which is to form your own lure bodies from scratch, shaping them out of blocks of wood, paint them yourself, and buy only the fittings that aren't practical to make, such as hooks and screw eyes. Almost all the control devices such as rudders that determine the plug's diving depth or keep it on the surface, and fins that cause it to zigzag or run in a straight line as it's retrieved. The techniques needed to produce these fittings are pretty thoroughly detailed in the preceding chapter. The disadvantage of starting plug fabrication from scratch is that you'll need tools. To offset that, these tools you probably already have handy, if you maintain any sort of home workshop at all, and the few you might not own are relatively inexpensive.

Being of a naturally impatient disposition, I can't see much virtue in writing two or three paragraphs telling you how to insert the threaded end of a screw eye in a predrilled hole in a plug and turn the eye until it's seated firmly. That's about the only job you'll be performing if you go the assembly route, aside from finishing, which will be covered later in this chapter. Let's shun unnecessary preliminaries and get down to the business of making plug bodies from scratch.

FORMING PLUG BODIES

A preliminary word of caution needs to be dropped. Unless you're a very good wood-carver or whittler and have a pretty fair knowledge of wood graining, there are some plug forms that you shouldn't try to duplicate by hand. These are the thin types with compound body curves of which Charley Helin's famous Flatfish is a typical example. Bodies of this kind that are created by hand present problems that the casual woodworker simply can't cope with. They are apt to shear along a grain-line unless they're very knowledgeably laid out on the blank, and have critical areas such as the leading edge, which must be shaved almost paper-thin.

In fact, most plugs having shapes similar to that of the Flatfish aren't made of wood any longer but are cast from plastic, usually in halves that

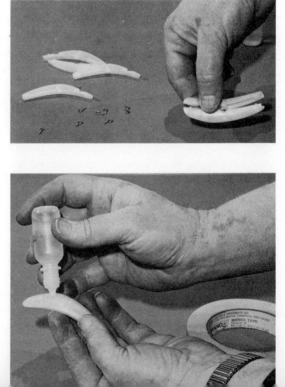

Plug bodies that have tricky compound curves are available in halves with interlocking nubs along their edges. They can be assembled at home and rigged with eyes and hooks.

An adhesive furnished with the forms dissolves the plastic momentarily so that the halves can be fused together. Press two halves together, leaving a tiny crack into which the adhesive dribbles, then push. No clamps or other pressure are required.

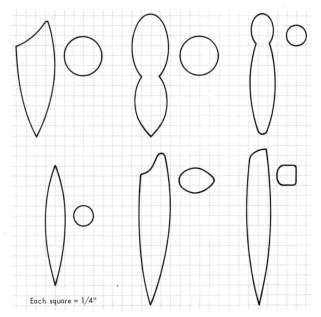

Each square = 1/4"

Templates are needed to get symmetrical bodies when making wooden plugs. To use these, rule off a piece of cardboard on squares of the scaled-up or scaled-down size required and transfer the curves with the squares as your guide. Cut the cardboard in halves along the centerline; press it to the work while you turn it. Combining curves produces bodies of many shapes.

are then joined together. They're available as kits, and with the kit you get a bottle of the joining liquid, which isn't a glue or adhesive but a solvent that actually melts the surface of the plastic and fuses the two halves of the plug into a single piece. If you're partial to this kind of plug, you're better advised to assemble kits than to try to reproduce their tricky curved bodies from a block of wood.

Rounded bodies are quite simple to make, and so are oval ones. To help you in producing them, template patterns of the most popular shapes accompany this chapter. To make the necessary templates, rule off a piece of cardboard into 1/4-inch squares and use the squares as a guide in reproducing the curves on the drawings. Cut the cardboard in halves, then cut out the outlined curves. To use the templates, press them to your work in progress and use them as a guide to whittling or sanding the wood block to the required shape. You can, of course, scale the sizes up or down by making larger or smaller squares on the cardboard; the curves will remain true.

If you're interested in saving time when forming plug bodies, use dowels for blanks; you can buy 3-foot long dowels from any lumberyard in diame-

A craft knife is your best tool for roughing in a wood block, but use the knife to which you're accustomed. Keep it sharp.

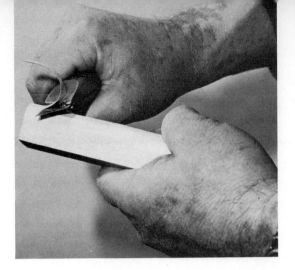

Quick, smooth shaving, especially of curves and end-grain, is easy with the Stanley Sur-Form tool shown. It's pulled rather than pushed, which gives you good control.

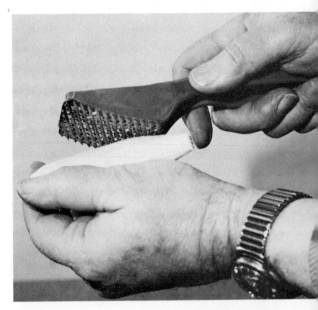

Use the template often as your plug takes on its finished shape.

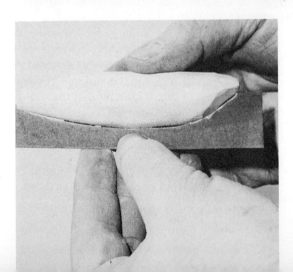

In the final finishing of a body plug, use fine sandpaper with a soft backing, such as sponge rubber, for a smooth surface.

ters of up to 1 or 1½ inches. If you'd rather save money, start with wood blocks; we've already seen where you can get them. You can also buy basswood blocks from many lure materials dealers.

For the sake of argument, let's say you choose to start with a wood block. Your first job is to reduce it to rough form with a knife or chisel; most lure makers find a knife more versatile in this operation. After forming a rough cylinder, true it up with a rasp or one of the Stanley SurForm tools shown in the illustration. If you have either an oscillating power sander or an arbor for your power drill that will accomodate sanding disks, use either of these to reduce your cylinder to its final form. A sanding drum is handy for making nose scoops and for fine hairline touch-up work.

Use the template as illustrated when your plug begins to reach the mid-point in forming. For the final stages of shaping, rely more on coarse sandpaper backed by a piece of soft material such as a small square of spongy plastic; the work will go more slowly, but there'll be less chance of making an uncorrectable mistake. When the plug is completed to your satisfaction, finish it off with fine sandpaper, such as 3M #140 garnet cabinet paper, then wet the wood and polish the plug with #440-grade wet-or-dry sandpaper. If the wood still feels fuzzy after you've used this paper, wet the wood and paper and go over it a second time. The better surface you provide now, the better the plug's finish will be.

You'll find it helpful and time-saving if you follow production-line techniques to a limited extent in plug making. That is, when you start to make plugs, plan to make several, and perform all similar operations on each plug before going on to the next process. Doing all your whittling, rasping, filing, rough sanding, and so forth on several plug bodies avoids the need for assembling tools and working supplies several times. About half the time put in on most craft jobs is spent getting a workbench set up, so if you do all the work required in each step on several plug bodies your time-savings will really mount up.

Mark the cut-lines for a waisted plug by rotating the body with one hand against a pencil held in the other.

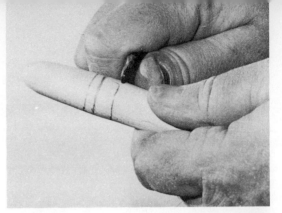

A knife file held like the pencil will score the centerline evenly and deeply.

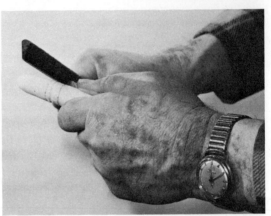

Rough in the taper by whittling to the centerline from each side.

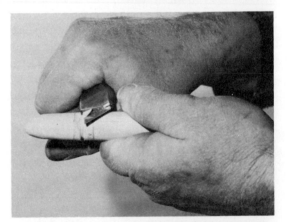

A triangular file completes the roughing in; then go to sandpaper, using the edge of the sanding block and rotating the work into the paper.

60

When forming a waisted plug, first reduce your wood block to a cylinder, or form the ends of a dowel. Then, use a pencil held firmly in one hand while rotating the plug along the lead with the other hand to mark the waist and the points above and below where the body taper begins. The sharp edge of a knife file makes quick work of scoring the cylinder; hold the file steady and revolve the work rather than passing the file over the dowel. This gives you much better control. After scoring the waistline, whittle the taper to it, working from the line to the scored groove of the waist. Finish roughing in the waistline with a triangular file and sand with narrow strips of fine sandpaper used like a shoeshine cloth while the plug body is held in a vise. This lets your sandpaper get right into the centerline of the waisted section.

If you want to make a jointed plug, simply cut the plug into two sections at the point where you want the joint to be, relieve the rear portion of the cut with a few file-strokes for maximum action, and join the two parts with linked screw eyes.

Cut nose scoops of the size that matches the plug body; there isn't any such thing as a "standard" pattern, so let your imagination be your guide. The important thing about these scoops is that they be attached to the plug body at the proper angle. You can do this in either of two ways. You can cut a slanting groove in the plug head and leave the scoop straight, or you can cut a groove in the head parallel to the plug's top and bottom and bend the scoop. Of the two, I think you'll find the slanting cut method the easier to work with.

There are three angles with which you want to be concerned when cutting grooves for scoops. A 20-degree angle will cause the plug to dive roughly 10 to 12 feet and run at about that depth when retrieved slowly. A 30-degree angle gives you a dive of about 20 feet, and the plug when retrieved slowly will run at about that depth, and a 40-degree angle will give you a 28- to 30-foot dive and retrieve depth. It must be understood that these depth figures are approximate at best and are based on a line eye that is approximately at right angles to the scoop. Form the line eye in the scoop holes from spinner wire.

After cutting the groove for the scoop, fit it in place, first marking the approximate angle at which the hook eye that anchors it must take to pass through the scoop's hole. Drill at this angle, then test by inserting the scoop in the groove and probing with a small-diameter wire to make sure the eye will take the desired path. If the hole passes this test, fit the scoop in and screw in the eye all the way, then back the eye out for most of its length, remove the scoop, and fill the groove with epoxy. Set the scoop in position, run the screw eye in, and set the plug aside for the glue to dry. When it's set up solid, scrape and sand around the groove area to remove any dribbles of epoxy, and the plug is ready to be painted after the scoop has been covered with masking tape.

Measure the depth of cut required for a nose scoop and mark the angle of the cut as well as the center hole screw.

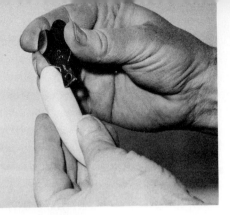

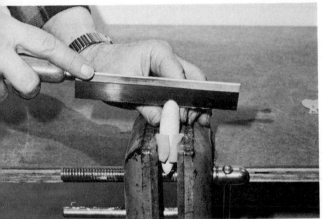

Use a fine-tooth saw to cut the groove for the scoop. Protect the body of the plug you've worked so hard to finish by cushioning the jaws of the vise.

Cradle and control the drill when making a pilot hole for the screw that anchors the nose scoop to keep the bit from going all the way through the plug's head.

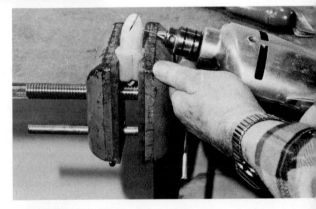

After testing the assembly, fill the groove into which the scoop will go with an epoxy or other waterproof metal-to-wood glue.

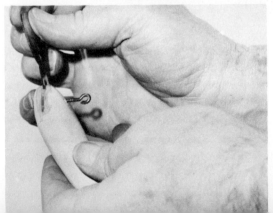

FINISHING PLUG BODIES

There are several kinds of finishes that give good results when used on lures, many of them the conventional enamels traditionally associated with wood finishing. However, you'll get a harder and more scratchproof finish with auto-body enamel, acrylic or epoxy enamel, put on over a flat under-coat. If you select traditional enamels, give the plug a final outer coat of acrylic or polyurethane varnish.

You can paint your plugs by spraying or dipping, dipping being by far the easier and more economical method. If you have the patience to wait while the dipped plug drains back into the container, you'll save a lot of paint. If you elect to use spray paints, you'll need a cabinet of some kind to protect your surroundings while spraying and to keep the plugs from ac-quiring dust motes while drying. Get two big corrugated cartons that have their lids still attached.

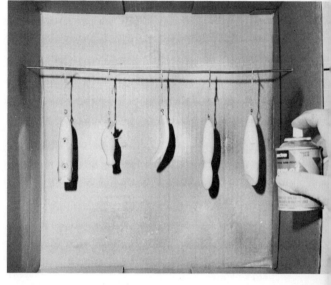

A cardboard carton fitted with a hanging rod protects surround-ings from spray paint and gives you a dust-free drying area. Hang the plugs by temporary eyes on a doubled cord; twist the cords so that the plugs will unwind as you spray to get a smooth, even finish.

For each of the cartons, cut a length of very stiff clothesline wire long enough to pass through the sides of the cartons and protrude 3 to 4 inches on the outside. Stack the cartons one atop the other with the tops facing your work area. The tops will be the doors, of course, and I find it's more convenient to have them swing upward, letting gravity and a strip of mask-ing tape keep them closed when required.

You now have a pair of spray-painting cabinets, one in which to paint, the other for drying. Remember, if you don't want a lot of plugs that are all the same color, you can spray-paint only one color at a time. The double cabinet arrangement makes it possible to spray several colors in quick suc-cession, transferring the painted plugs to the drying box when you switch colors. Your dipped plugs can also be hung in the drying box to keep dust specks from settling on them.

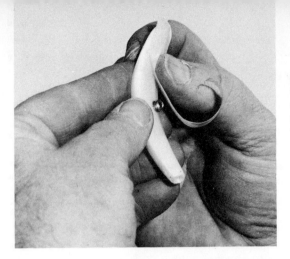

Mask the plugs as required for a two-tone finish; be sure one color is bone-dry before putting on masking tape to shield it while you spray the second color or trim color.

To get the best possible finish requires some work. First, undercoat your plugs by dipping or spraying and let them dry bone-hard. Using wet-or-dry sandpaper wet, go over them lightly. Wipe them dry and inspect them for rough spots; remove these with a dampened cloth dipped in rottenstone or pumice. When you're sure the undercoat is as smooth as it's possible to get it, apply the enamel.

You will, of course, have masked off any sections of any plug for which you plan a two-tone finish. The second color is applied after the first has dried hard and you've removed the old masking tape and put fresh tape on to cover the first color. There are all kinds of patterns that can be produced by using masking tape judiciously: fins, skeleton stripes, half-and-half, almost any combination you wish. Spraying is the best method for producing multicolor effects, for no matter how firmly you press masking tape onto a plug, a bit of color's going to ooze under the tape at the edges if you dip it.

Spraying is the method used when giving a plug a scale finish. There's a special scale net offered by most tackle suppliers that is used for this effect, and some specialty fabric shops stock an almost identical nylon mesh material. The holes in this material may be a bit larger than those in the small-mesh nets sold by tackle dealers, but you'll get essentially the same scale effect.

Everyone has his own ideas about the best method to use in giving lures a scale finish. Some recommend putting the mesh in a frame and suspending

For a sparkling finish, mask off part of the plug, give the unmasked area a shot of clear acrylic spray and roll it in glitter dust while still wet. Protect with a second coat over the glitters after the first coat is dry.

There are several ways to use the mesh net that gives plugs a scale finish. The easiest is to wrap the plug in a strip of the mesh and hold it with old clothespins. Hang the plug so that the spray hits only the desired areas.

the plug several inches from the frame, letting the paint spray go through the mesh to strike the plug. The method I find most successful—and easiest—is simply to wrap a piece of the mesh around the plug, hold it in place with clothespins, and hang the plug so that the spray will hit it only across its upper portion. Take the mesh off at once, peeling it carefully from the plug to avoid smearing, and hang the plug up to dry. You'll produce a more pronounced effect if you use a sharply contrasting color such as yellow in base-coating the plug, and a top coat of greenish brown or reddish brown to form the "scales."

If you want to take the time and trouble to do so, you can fit your plugs with glass eyes by countersinking small cavities on either side of the front and gluing the eyes in. Or, you can use decal eyes, which cost next to nothing and are no trouble to apply. You can fit plugs with tiny propellers fore or aft or at both ends; just be sure to use a nose washer between the line eye and the end of the plug so that the propeller will spin easily.

You can also decorate your plugs with painted eyes or stripes put on with a small brush, or with strips of lure tape. Since I'm basically lazy, I like the tape decorations because they're so easy to apply. Put them on, of course, before giving your plugs their finish coat of clear acrylic or urethane varnish.

Always wait until all painting and decorating are finished before fitting plugs with hardware. If you predrill holes before the paint goes on, stick toothpicks or slivers of wood in them to keep them open during the painting process. If you're very confident of your ability to use a small bit in your drill with enough control to keep from drilling right through the plug, use your electric drill. If you have any doubts, chuck the small wire-gauge drill used into a pin vise and do the job by hand; it takes only a minute or so, and you run no risk of marring a finish that's been so carefully put on.

Finally, take the same imaginative approach to making plugs that you used when making lures. Don't be afraid to experiment. If you do find a better plug, the path anglers will beat to your door will look like a six-lane freeway!

6

Soft-bodied Lures

As we saw in the introductory chapter, there are three groups of lures in this family. The dominant group is that made from soft plastic molded into the shapes of worms, grubs, frogs, crayfish, and other aquatic creatures; the second is a relatively small group, consisting of lures made by threading hooks through hollow rubber or plastic tubing; and the third is a borderline group, namely jigs, which while having hard heads have very soft bodies or tails.

Molded or cast lures have been around a while; I fished soft-bodied rubber minnows for bass in the late 1940s. They were made in Europe, closely imitated several kinds of live minnows and were quite effective when trolled or cast behind a tiny spinner. Soft-bodied lures didn't really flower until about the mid-1960s, though, when tales began to seep out of the South and Southwest about how bottom-feeding lunker bass, which probably hadn't seen an artificial lure since their fingerling days, were hitting big purple plastic worms with an eagerness that came close to ferocity. Suddenly, an assortment of plastic molded lures became required equipment in everybody's tacklebox.

There's no question about the effectiveness of these lures; they do what fishermen have been trying to do since angling first began: imitate natural foods successfully enough to fool the fish. That they do this with plastic instead of fur, feathers, metal, or wood isn't the point; the point is that soft-bodied lures are now an important part of the angling scene.

More and more fishermen have started molding their own, and the molds available have multiplied accordingly in variety and size. One firm alone, the Limit Manufacturing Company, which specializes in molded plastic lure supplies, offers over sixty worm shapes in sizes ranging from 10-inch monsters designed to attract big bass down to tiny 2-inch grubs for panfish. The firm offers molds for so many other shapes as well that the soft-bodied lure man will never lack a new shape with which to experiment.

By the mid-1970s, there were quite probably more fishermen who were molding lures of plastic than there were who worked on hard-bodied lures and tied flies. There are good reasons why soft-bodied lures hit the make-'em-yourself jackpot. The investment in equipment is modest, the process is easy to learn, and the working time involved is very short. In an hour, a steady worker can cast a hundred or more of these plastic forms — and salvage old battered ones by remelting them as he makes new ones.

If molded plastic lures have any drawbacks, it's the frequency with which they must be replaced. They are, in the angler's frame of reference, quite vulnerable. Short-striking fish pull them apart, and when a heavy fish is being played, one that requires a lot of time to bring to net, the lure is often sawed up by the abrasive monofilament of line or leader. Since these lures are fished on the bottom most of the time, they're prone to snagging, and, as is the case with many soft plastics, they're very susceptible to damage by ultraviolet light. Prolonged exposure makes the plastic "bleed," or become brittle or mushy — depending on the formula.

But these lures have more going for them than against them. Aside from the fact that they *do* work, the fisherman molding his own can make the plastic softer or stiffer, can color it to any shade that's locally hot at the moment and can also add to the liquid plastic being heated a compound that fills the lure with bubbles and makes it a semifloater.

Using figures current at the time this is written, you will repay yourself for your investment in molds after casting seventy to seventy-five large worms or their equivalent in other shapes. This figure is based on the use of a three-cavity mold costing about $4.00; naturally, each mold must produce the equivalent of those seventy to seventy-five worms before your

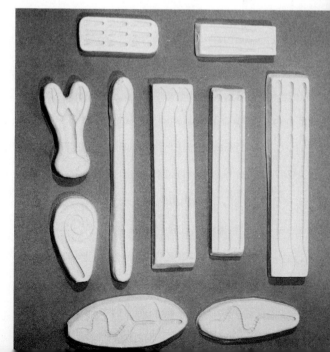

These are just a few samples of the hundreds of mold shapes and sizes available to the angler wanting to mold his own soft-bodied lures. The molds are infinitely reusable.

cost per casting drops below what you'd pay for the same number at prevailing retail prices. Once you've gone past the break-even point, your saving per lure will be about 50 percent; you can make two lures for the same amount of money you'd pay for one across the retail counter. The figures include casting plastic and dye in addition to the molds but do not include heating costs nor take into account the salvage value of broken lures that are remelted.

MOLDING PLASTIC LURES

Molding these soft-bodied lures requires an absolute minimum of equipment and time, and no special skill of any sort. In addition to some kind of heat source, a kitchen range, a gasoline or LP-gas camp stove, even an old wood-burning stove if you have one, you need only a pot, a stick to stir with, and the molds themselves. If you want to, you can make your own molds from plaster of Paris; this procedure will be described and pictured later in this chapter.

Equipment and supplies for casting plastic lures. I use an old LP-gas-fueled camp stove in my workshop; a small can of fuel provides enough for three average pouring sessions. Depending on your plans, you'll need the casting liquid, softener or hardener, dye, and scent, if you want to flavor the lures. A foaming agent is also available. Tools are a couple of melting utensils and a stirrer.

Molds used in casting plastic lures require no preheating, no treating with a mold-release compound, and no advance preparation. The plastic used comes in liquid form and must be heated at a low, even temperature for twenty to twenty-five minutes with regular stirring. With too high a heat or too little stirring, the plastic will burn and deposit tiny to big black flakes in the compound. Your best bet is to work with a small quantity of plastic, especially when you first begin learning the process. A half-cup of the liquid will make about twenty-five to thirty lures, depending on the size of the molds used.

Line up the molds as close to the heat source as possible, for the plastic cools very quickly. A viscous milky-looking liquid in its original state, it becomes first thick and gummy, then translucent and syrupy as it heats. Color is added during the heating process, a couple of drops of either translucent or opaque dye per pint. As soon as the casting material has passed through the stage of gummy thickness and become the consistency of a good grade of pancake syrup, you're ready to fill the molds.

Quick work at this point is essential. The mold cavities should be filled in a single steady pouring, for the plastic sets up almost at once. When you pour, don't worry too much about spills, and don't hesitate to fill the mold cavities level-full. Spills don't adhere to any substance except cloth, though if you spill hot plastic on a newspaper page it will pick up the ink from the page when pulled away from the paper. As soon as all the mold cavities are filled, put the melting pot back on the heat source to keep the plastic ready for the next pouring.

When the plastic's ready to pour, it becomes a smooth, syrupy, translucent liquid. Set the molds close together; you must pour fast, for the plastic sets up quickly when taken off heat.

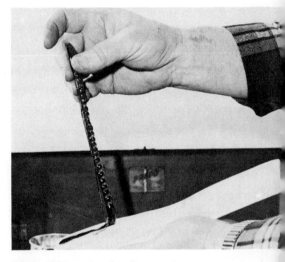

Within thirty seconds after pouring you can pull out the forms; the plastic's still warm, but not too hot to handle.

This can take place almost at once. The plastic poured into the molds becomes firm within thirty to forty-five seconds and can be handled within sixty to seventy-five seconds; even though it's still warm to the touch, it's not too warm to be pulled from the mold cavities. Some makers recommend putting the newly filled molds in water to speed cooling, but I haven't found this necessary. However, it's a shrewd idea to drop the freshly cast forms in a pan of cool water, for they'll set up fully much more quickly if this is done.

After scoring, the blobs pull away, parting at the score line.

As soon as a mold is emptied it can be refilled, unless it's been dunked in water to cool it. If this has been done, the mold must be thoroughly dried before being used again, or the plastic will sputter and form blotches when it touches any moisture left clinging to the cavities. The plastic must also be kept hot and must be stirred to prevent burning while the molds are being emptied in preparation for the next pour. If the pouring pan isn't returned to the heat source, the plastic in it will begin to set up, and your next pouring must be delayed until it can be remelted.

After the freshly cast forms are cool, they can be trimmed at the edges where small beads of plastic may have collected due to the molds having been overfilled. Just run a sharp knife along the edge of the cast form where these overpour blobs are located, then pull the excess away. It's easier to score the plastic and pull it away than it is to try to cut it off cleanly, for the material will follow even the sharpest knife unless the lightest pressure is placed on the blade. Toss the trimmed-off blobs, as well as any plastic that's been spilled, back into the pot to be remelted. And, if you've botched filling a mold cavity, throw your mistakes back in for melting and repouring. As far as I've been able to learn, there's no practical limit to the number of times the plastic material can be melted and reused.

Open-mold casting is the quickest, easiest, and most economical method you can use. There are also injection molds available that produce a fully rounded form, whereas forms cast in open molds will always have flat bottoms. The injection molds, however, are very slow to use. They are made in two parts, the injecting plunger and the mold itself. In use, the two-piece mold is clamped shut, the plunger container filled, and the plastic forced into the mold with the plunger. Since the plastic sets up as quickly in these

70

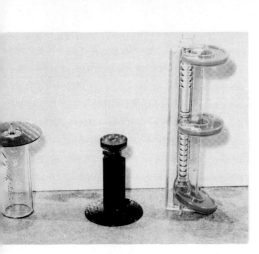

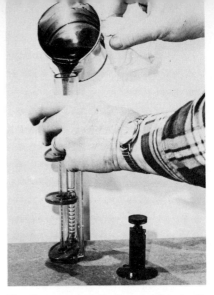

Injection molds produce full-round forms and consist of three units: container (left), plunger or piston (center), and mold (right). Lock rings slide on the mold to hold its halves together.

The first step in injection molding is sitting the container on the mold and filling it with liquid plastic.

Working quickly, fit the piston in the container and press on it to drive the plastic into the mold.

Almost as soon as the container-piston assembly can be laid aside, the mold is ready to be opened and the lure removed.

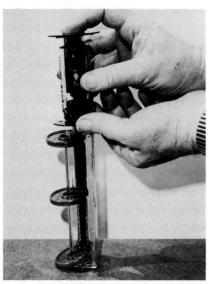

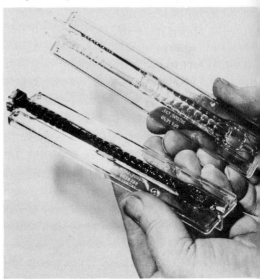

To make your own molds, fill the top of a box or any similar shallow container with plaster of Paris.

Press the models into the liquid plaster, let set.

When the plaster is fully dry, remove the models. The mold is ready for use, but be very sure it's bone-dry, since moisture will cause bubbled surfaces on castings made in a wet mold.

molds as it does in the open type, the filled mold can be opened at once and the form removed, and the mold is again ready for use.

Opening, emptying, and reclosing the injection mold is time-consuming, and so is the job of clearing the plunger device of hardened plastic; invariably, a half-teaspoon of plastic will harden in the bottom of the plunger well, filling the nozzle through which it flows to the mold, and this residue must be cleared away before the plunger can be used again. In relation to open-mold casting, the injection process still has some catching-up to do.

Molds represent the greatest initial cost to the lure maker interested in casting soft-bodied lures. If you want to cast a variety of lure shapes, you can quickly run up a sizable investment in rubber molds. But—you can very easily make your own molds, as long as you have one specimen of the lure you want to reproduce to serve as a model. Making your own mold is a five-minute job, though there's a period of several hours—preferably overnight—while you wait for the mold to harden.

To make your own molds, you need a shallow container, such as the lid of a shoe box, and a 2-pound package of plaster of Paris; the plaster will cost you about 45¢ a pound at lumberyards and craft stores. Put the powdered plaster into a large can or other container, stir in enough water to make a creamy, thick paste, pour the plaster into the boxtop, filling it level-full, then press into the plaster the forms you want to reproduce. Let the plaster set up fully, overnight if possible. Remove the forms used for models, and your molds are ready to be used. You cannot tell the difference between forms cast in these homemade molds and those that come from commercial molds, and the processes involved in using the plaster molds are exactly the same as those followed when using commercial molds.

There are all sorts of things you can do with plastic lures at the time you're making them. First, you have a wide choice of dyes with which to color the lures: purple, white, red, yellow, and black in opaque dyes; blue, red, green, yellow, brown, wine, grape, orange, and chartreuse in translucent dyes; red, green, blue, pink, silver, and gold in fluorescent dyes. To my knowledge, nobody's conducted any sort of piscine poll to find out which color is most appealing to fish, but bass fishermen swear by purple and black, and trout fishermen by translucent brown, the shade that best reproduces a worm's color in its natural or live state.

In addition to single-color lures, you can cast multicolor shapes. This means using a separate melting pot for each color you want to add to your lures. Simply fill the molds to the halfway mark with the color you want to be at the top of your lure, and before this pour sets up firmly, fill the molds with the second color. If you want a half-and-half effect fore and aft in a lure, use a small piece of cardboard as a dam, fill the cavity with color one, remove the dam at once and pour color two. Multicolor molding means that you can, for instance, mold frogs with green backs and yellow bellies, or any other natural shading you wish.

Fitting a Soft-bodied Lure with Hooks

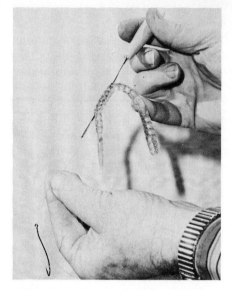

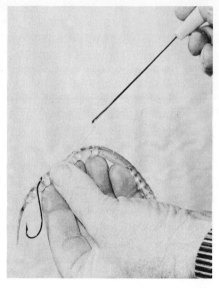

1. Use a tool similar to the saltwater commercial fisherman's bait needle. Begin by snelling a hook to the end of a piece of leader material about 8 to 10 inches longer than the lure you're fitting. Push the snelling tool into the lure and through the center of its body, bringing the eye out at the point where you want the bend of the back hook to be. Thread the monofil through the eye.

2. Pull the tool out, bringing with it the doubled monofil and pulling the bottom hook into place. Snell on the second hook; make your tie at the point where the eye of hook #2 will be after it's in the lure's body.

4. Pull out the tool, bringing the doubled monofil with it and pulling the second hook into the lure's body.

3. Push the tool in from the head of the lure, through the center of its body, bringing the eye out where you want the bend of hook #2 to be. Thread the monofil through the eye of the tool.

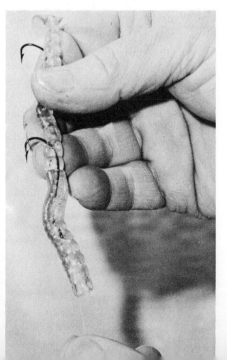

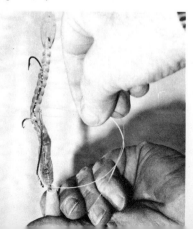

You can also add scents to your lures by mixing in the appropriate blend while the plastic is melting. You've a choice of anise, strawberry, cinnamon, lime, lemon, and grape. Anise holds first place among the soft-bodied lure fishermen with whom I've discussed this matter, and they're unanimous in swearing that it does increase the effectiveness of these lures, especially when bottom fishing.

The use of hardening, softening, and foaming compounds has already been mentioned, but nothing's yet been said about stirring some glitter dust in the plastic after it's melted to give a twinkly effect to the finished lures. And, of course, the multicolor technique already described can be used to put squiggles or designs of one or more colors on a lure; just run a wavy line of the melted plastic along the bottom of the mold before filling it with plastic of a contrasting shade.

Plastic lures must be fitted with hooks, and since these lures are generally fished deep, usually on the bottom, they're prone to snag when an outside rigging is used. There's a simple snelling tool that makes it easy and practical to rig hooks and the leader material joining them inside the body of these lures. The tool is similar to the baiting needles used to rig eels fished in saltwater.

Start the rigging job by snelling a bait hook on one end of a piece of leader material about 6 or 8 inches longer than the lure being rigged. Push the snelling tool into the body of the lure at the point where you want the barb of the forward hook to be, and push the needle through the lure at the point where you want the barb of the back hook to be. Thread the leader material into the rigging tool and pull the tool out of the lure, bringing the doubled leader with it and pulling the back hook into the body of the lure. Attach the front hook to the leader material, spacing the snell so that the barb will be in the right place when the hook is pulled into the lure.

Push the needle into the lure from its head and through the center of the body, to come out and be threaded with leader at the point where the barb of the front hook will be. Pull the tool out of the lure, bringing the doubled leader material with it and pulling the front hook into the body of the lure. It takes a lot less time to do all this than it does to read about it, and the result is a lure with all hooks and leader inside the body, where they won't snag as easily as they would outside.

MAKING SURGE LURES

Now, let's move on to other members of the soft-bodied lure family, specifically the "surge lures," as they've come to be called, the name deriving from the fact that the originals were made from short lengths of latex rubber surgical tubing.

Surge lures are the simplest of all types to construct. All you need to make them is a bit of tubing — and now these lures are being made not only from opaque rubber surgical tubing, but from various kinds of plastic industrial tubing—a hook, and either some spinner wire or a split ring and a swivel.

Start by aligning your components on a block of wood so that you can see where to cut the tubing. Place the end of the tubing at the midpoint of the swivel and cut it at a slant; the bottom edge of the back of the tubing should be just a fraction of an inch longer than the hook's bend. Cut a slit in the piece of tubing that will form the lure's body at the bottom of the short side of the slanted end.

Tube lures are made by cutting a length of surgical rubber or plastic tubing to the proper length. Laying out the components as illustrated makes it easy to gauge where to cut. The rear end of the tubing is cut slantwise to keep the hook's point down; a small slit at the bottom helps do this, too.

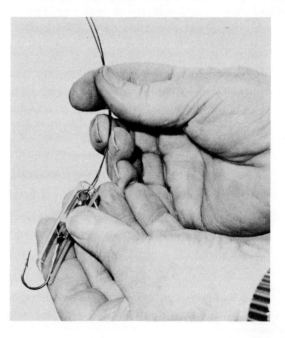

Assemble the hook and swivel—a split ring is the easiest way—and with a loop of wire pull the swivel through the tubing. Transparent tubing is used for photo purposes; it's also popular for lures, clear or colored.

Twist a loop of wire at the bottom of the swivel, around the outside of the lure. You may have to make V cuts around the front rim of the tubing if it has thick walls, to tighten the wire enough. Just be sure the wire doesn't keep the swivel from working.

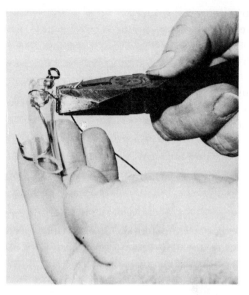

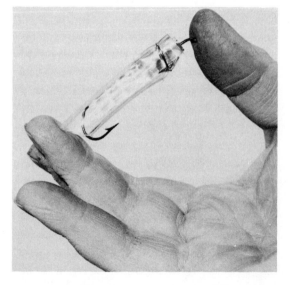

A transparent tube lure with tape inside is very flashy indeed.

Assemble the interior, connecting the swivel and hook with a split ring or a short length of spinner wire eyed at both ends. Double a piece of wire or heavy monofil and use it to pull the hook assembly through the tubing. Force the bend of the hook into the slit cut at the bottom of the tubing. Pull the tubing tightly around the split ring, making sure the swivel can turn freely, by twisting a piece of spinner wire around the front end of the tubing. If the walls of plastic tubing are very thick, cut several Vs in the front rim so that the tubing can be pulled snugly into place.

Don't let the austere appearance of tube lures fool you; for some reason, they attract their fair share of strikes.

This is the basic surge lure. It can be modified in many ways. A sinker crimped on a long-shanked hook and covered with shiny lure tape makes a very flashy lure in transparent plastic tape. When regular rubber surgical tubing is used, it can be skirted with a rubber lure skirt at the head, or a tiny willow-leaf spinner can be put in an eye formed in the spinner wire that crimps the tubing at the front. Mylar trailers can be attached to the bend of the hook, or strips of Mylar pulled in by the tie-off wire at the head of the lure. The back of the tubing itself can be slashed to make a wriggling skirt. The number of variations is limited only by your ingenuity in figuring out how to add attractors to these relatively new members of the soft-bodied lure family.

One variation on the surge lure is to cover hooks with multicolored lengths of small-diameter tubing, holding the tubing in place with brass beads crimped on the hook fore and aft of the tubing. If a deep-running lure is desired, crimp a couple of split shot on the shank of the hook before slipping the tubing in place. There are a number of colors of this small-diameter plastic tubing available, in fluorescent as well as regular. It takes about two minutes to put one of these small-sized surge lures together, and their cost is about 1½¢ plus whatever you've paid for the hook used. Unweighted or lightly weighted, these lures can be fished with a fly rod if you choose.

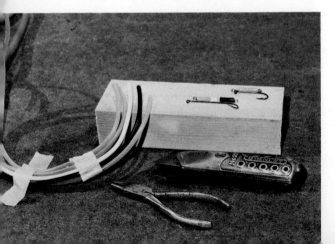

Small tube lures can be made from varicolored plastic tubing held in place by brass beads crimped fore and aft of the tubing. You are limited only by the number of colors—about ten, some fluorescent—in which this tubing is available.

MAKING JIGS

Finally we arrive at the third group in the soft-bodied lure family: jigs. Their classification in this family may cause you to raise a questioning eyebrow, but jigs present a peculiar problem; they have hard heads but soft skirts or bodies and are neither plugs nor flies. They aren't dominant enough to deserve being categorized as a separate lure family, so their inclusion in the soft-bodied family seems to be the most practical compromise.

Jigs are in fact gaining an increasingly important place in angling. Once used primarily for ice fishing, they've now been found to work equally well in all other seasons of the year and are being used as trolling and casting lures as well as being danced up and down through a hole in the ice.

In a photograph quite a number of pages back we saw the variety of jig heads that are available from just one supplier, and other dealers have other forms in about as great a variety. Molds for all these and other forms are available if you decide to cast your own jig heads. That decision is one you must make, based on your use of this kind of lure plus the relative costs of buying ready-cast heads or casting your own.

Figures that I developed for this book, using figures current at the time of writing, show that you must cast roughly fifty jigs with ¼-ounce heads before your cost drops below that of commercially manufactured heads. This break-even point was computed on the basis of your investment being limited to one three-cavity mold and using an old scrounged-up pot for melting, plus the cost of materials, figuring lead at the scrap price of about 20¢ per pound and hooks at current prices. In other words, once you've cast those fifty jigs, your cost per jig head drops to about 50 percent of the cost of the one you buy.

Of course, if you go deluxe, with a thermostatically controlled melting pot and similar accessories, and buy several multiple-cavity molds, your break-even point's going to come only after you've cast a lot more than fifty jig heads. The economics here boil down to how many jigs you'll use over a season of fishing. If you use them regularly and fish often, the cost of replacing lost jigs mounts up. If you fish jigs only occasionally, you're probably ahead if you just buy the precast heads and add your own skirting, and do your own painting of the heads.

Casting lead is only slightly different from casting plastic. You'll be working with higher temperatures and will want to be very careful not to inhale fumes from the molten metal, but basically the process of casting into a mold is the same whether the molten material poured into the cavities is plastic or metal.

Lead can come from a variety of sources: target ranges, if you can beat reloaders to the sandbags; service stations that do a lot of tire work and have discarded wheel weights to dispose of; plumbing shops; scrapyards; even newspaper offices and print shops that still use linotypes. The hooks you use must, of course, be of the right size and shape to fit your molds.

Melt the lead in any kind of battered old pot you can pick up; just be sure the pot's got a pouring lip. As the metal liquifies and turns from dull grey to silver, impurities will rise to the surface, and these—called dross—must be skimmed off. An old tablespoon makes a very satisfactory skimmer.

Jig molds have slots in which the hooks are placed, and as already noted, the hooks must be of the correct shape and size to fit these slots. When the hooks are in position and the mold is closed, it's then held upright while the hot lead is poured in through funnel-shaped holes in the top. The lead sets up in thirty to forty-five seconds, and the mold can then be opened and the jigs removed. They're still very hot, so handle them with pliers.

Casting a Jig Head

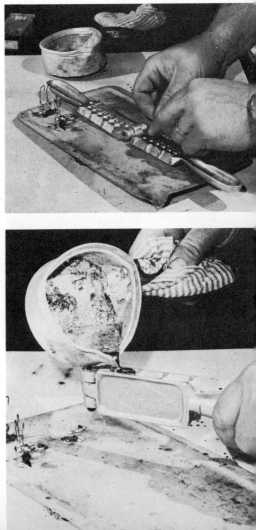

1. Skim off the dross from the melted lead (above). The skimmings must be discarded; they're useless.

2. Put hooks of the correct kind into the slots provided in the mold (above right). The hooks must match the mold.

3. Hooks in place, the mold is held upright and molten lead poured into the funnel-shaped openings of the cavities (right). Only two of this mold's six cavities are being used in the pictures.

Even the best molds will allow some seepage of molten metal at the edges of the cavities; this forms a thin, ragged fringe around the head and must be trimmed off. It's called "flash," if you really care about such technicalities. The holes into which the molten metal is poured are technically known as "sprue holes," hence the name "sprue" given to the little funnel-shaped blobs that the jigs wear on their heads when they first come out of the mold, the blobs being caused by lead that remains in the sprue holes after pouring. Flash and sprue must both be trimmed away; electrician's wire cutters are the easiest tool to use for this chore, which is done after the jigs get cool enough to be handled comfortably.

4. A half-minute after pouring, the mold can be opened and the castings removed (above). The lead's hot, so use pliers.

5. Sprue and flash (see text for definitions) are trimmed off with electrician's wire cutters (above right). A file may be used on thin flash.

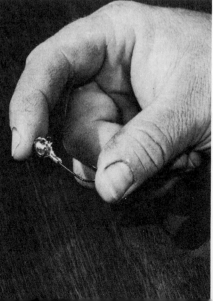

6. Cool enough to handle, the jig is ready for painting and skirting (right).

Painting the jig heads can be done most easily and economically by dipping. If you dip, the only masking required is the line eye, while if you spray-paint, line eye and hook must both be protected with masking tape. Of course, you can paint the heads with a brush and there won't be any masking to worry about. After the jigs have been painted, add eyes or stripes or whatever other decoration your fancy dictates, then put skirts on to cover the hooks. Incidentally, those rubbery compounds into which tool handles are dipped to insulate and protect users' hands make excellent jig-head coverings. These liquids are available in several colors and give a jig head a semisoft coating that seems to help reduce snagging.

Dipping is the easy way to paint jig heads; mask the hook eye with tape before dipping to save work later.

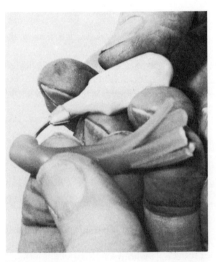

Skirts made of latex tubing can be cut to fit precisely and fringed at the back to wave and wiggle.

As for the skirting, most jig fishermen favor one of three types of skirts: a ready-made rubber or plastic slip-on fringe, surgical tubing, or a tied-on skirt of feathers or dyed artificial polar bear hair. The first two types of skirts require no effort except slipping over the hook, though if you want to you can trim the tubing into a sort of coarse fringe. A fur or feather skirt is really a fly-tying operation, and if you want a fancy skirt on your jigs, consult Part 2 of this book. But if you just want a simple skirt, here's how to put it on.

First, lay a foundation by wrapping the channel beneath the jig head evenly with coarse thread—a #5 fly-tying thread is easy to handle and covers quickly. Coat the thread with fly head cement, and while the adhesive is still tacky roll a layer of fur or place a half-dozen saddle hackles on the thread and wrap over them the length of the channel. Trim off any excess material that sticks up over the jig head. Have a 2-inch loop of thread handy, lay it on the wrapped portion with the closed end toward the head, and take about three or four more turns with the wrapping thread over the loop. Cut the wrapping thread, leaving an inch or so of extra length, put the end of the wrapping thread into the loop, pull the ends of the looped thread to bring the wrapping thread under those last few turns,

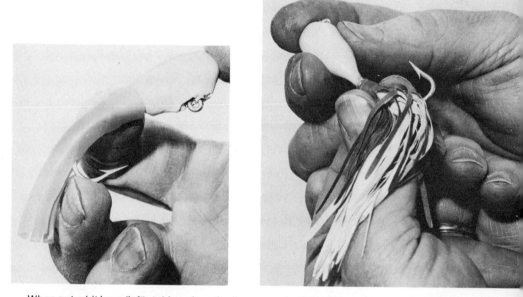

When cut a bit long (left), tubing gives the jig a curved, shrimplike appearance. Be sure to hold the jig with the point upward (right), when fitting rubber skirt, so that fringe will part and allow you to see hook, avoid accident.

and trim off the end. Then put on another coat of cement over the wrap. If you want further details, you'll find them in Part 2.

As you've seen while going through this chapter, in fact by going through the whole of Part 1, making lures can be a time-eating hobby. But it can also be a rewarding one to the fisherman who wants to try out his own ideas, and it can certainly save money. Besides, how could you find a better way to fill those long winter days between the end of the football season and the beginning of baseball?

PART TWO

HOW TO TIE FLIES

7

Flies, Fish, and Fishermen

AMONG THE WORD GAMES people used to play before television turned parlor games into a display of public exhibitionism there was one in which a player challenged the others to explain to him a totally foreign concept. The challenger might say, for instance: "I am an aborigine; I have never seen fire, never eaten cooked food, know nothing about metals or any other aspect of civilization. Explain to me what a frying pan is." Try that out in your own mind; it's a tougher challenge than you might think.

Every writer who sets out to explain procedures associated with a craft or skill must assume that his book will reach some readers who know absolutely nothing about the subject on which he's writing. So—before we ever put a hook in the tying vise or wax a length of thread or even think of looking at the gaudy bits of silk, wool, fur, and feathers that collect on a fly tier's bench, it seems wise to spend a bit of time on explanatory preliminaries. This involves reviewing some data that are old hat to expert fishermen but are perhaps new to those coming lately to the sport. If you classify yourself as either a veteran or an expert angler, feel free to skim or skip those paragraphs or pages that repeat what you already know.

Technically, all fishing flies fall into one of only two categories: dry and wet. Dry flies float, wet flies sink. Dry flies also sink sometimes when they're not supposed to, and when fishermen don't want them to, but that's one of the things this book may show you how to avoid.

Shortly after the dry fly was born in the 1850s, specialization began to set in, and it has proliferated through the years. Today we not only need to consider dry and wet flies separately but also must devote individual attention to subfamilies. In this section, however, we'll deal first with flies in general and review the tools needed to tie them, the materials used, and the procedures common to all kinds of flies. Then, we'll go into a bit of detail on the individual categories and look at the special materials and methods called for in tying them.

If you're just beginning to get interested in fly tying as an extension of fly fishing, this general, rather untechnical preamble probably won't bother you as much as it will the veterans. I'm sure some of them will object, because fly fishermen are the most contentious of all the angling fraternity. For years I've suspected that a few tie their own flies not just because they enjoy doing it, but to give them ammunition to use in their arguments with other fly fishermen.

Seriously, though, there are many very good reasons for fly tying, among them being economy and challenge. At current prices for good hand-tied flies you can assemble the equipment and materials needed to tie two hundred flies, ten each of twenty different patterns, for almost exactly what you'd pay for sixty well-tied flies, five each of twelve different patterns. To most anglers, though, the economy is less important than the challenge involved. This is the same challenge faced by every fisherman who makes his own lures, but to fly fishermen it seems more important to prove, by taking fish on flies they've tied themselves, that they're smarter than the fish. This, of course, is something every angler doubts from time to time.

We must go back nearly two thousand years to find the first description of tying a fishing fly. Claudius Aelianus, whom you met on the first page of this book, detailed very precisely the manner in which anglers tied a fly to imitate a beelike insect on which trout fed in the Astraeus River. Which stream in the area along the border between modern Greece and Bulgaria bore that name in Aelianus's time, I do not know, but I'm sure any modern fly tier would be able to produce a fly following his description of the manner in which anglers "lap a lock of reddish wool around the hook, and to the wool add two cock's feathers, which grow under the wattle and are brought to the proper color with wax." The fly he described is still being tied; today, we call it the Red Hackle.

Modern fly fishermen and tiers are the fortunate heirs to work done over a span of two thousand years by individuals gifted with more than ordinary powers of observation and deduction. Starting with Aelianus, the list of contributors to the art should include Dame Juliana Berners and Izaak Walton; Pritchard and Marryat and Skues, who contributed largely to the development of wet flies; Pulham, who suggested that a fly could be floated as well as being fished underwater; and those who followed Pulham: Halford, LaBranche, Hewitt, Gordon, Wulff, Leonard, Cross, Schwiebert, and scores of others. This paragraph would become a book in itself if I tried to list all the fishermen of yesterday and today who have made important contributions to the creation of more effective flies.

Though there are more names omitted from the list above than are included, the point is made. From the beginning of fly fishing, interested anglers have been observing streams and lakes, fish and the insects they feed on, in efforts to establish definitive theories that can be applied to the sport. They are still doing so today, and there are now so many theories old and new that are still being tested and debated that you have a wide choice in selecting the theories you will accept or reject.

All theories about fly fishing are valid up to the point of being provable at one time or another. If you've been around fly fishermen at all, you'll know what the theories are. If you're just getting your waders wet in what can with equal accuracy be described as an art, a craft, a sport, or a life-style, now's the time for you to learn these theories, since they'll inevitably influence your fly tying. For the record, then, let's look at the twelve schools of thought or belief into which the fly-fishing fraternity can be divided. To the best of my recollection, these beliefs have never been codified before, and I'm setting them down in the order in which they pop into my mind, not necessarily in the order of their prevalence or popularity.

First, there are the dry-fly purists. They will fish nothing except floating flies, regardless of wind or weather, regardless of season, in defiance of reason and experience.

Next come wet-fly purists, who swear that the only effective fly is the sunken fly. They're outnumbered by the dry-fly addicts, but equally vehement in support of their philosophy.

Nymph purists are a subclan of the wet-fly school; they scorn wings and feathers, and fish only detailed imitations of aquatic grubs.

There is a sizable school of fly fishermen who adhere only to one rule: "Bright day, bright fly; dark day, dark fly." They aren't meticulous in their choice of pattern as long as the hue of the fly agrees with the hue of the sky.

One school of fly fishermen insists that presentation of the fly is more important than type, color, or pattern.

Opposing them is the school that places pattern first in importance and relegates presentation to second or third place.

A substantial number of fly fishermen maintain that neither pattern nor presentation is as important as size; their theory is that as long as you cast flies with big, bulky bodies fish, being perennially hungry, will strike.

On the other side of the fence are anglers who point out that fat-bodied insects are in the minority, and that slim, streamlined flies look more realistic to the fish.

Many fly fishermen think it's futile to fish unless you can offer a fly resembling insects present in quantity at the time you're on the stream; they are impelled to "match the hatch" and often spend more time at streamside tying flies than they do fishing.

Some wet-fly fishermen hold to the belief that fish are color-blind, and that consequently a fly's shape is more important than its color.

Opposing views are held by another group; they maintain color is of paramount importance and always test their tying materials under water to check the effect of refraction on the colors.

A substantial number of dry-fly fishermen believe that the only important factor in dry-fly fishing is the dot pattern made by the fly's hackle on the surface of the water; they theorize that fish will strike only if the dot pattern matches that of a natural insect.

There are probably a few schools of fly-fishing thought that I've overlooked or forgotten. In listing the foregoing I'm not ridiculing or poking fun at the very studious and serious anglers who espouse any theory about fly fishing. The funny and frustrating thing to the fly tier is that all the theories are right part of the time, and all of them are wrong part of the time, and nobody knows why. I've seen most of the foregoing theories proved and disproved, and I have tested a number of them with my own flies during the many years when I fished flies almost exclusively and had plenty of time in which to experiment.

None of the theories I've ever tested has worked out more than 50 percent of the time, which is simply random odds. The theories about flies bring to mind the old gag question: "If you toss a coin and it comes up heads ninety-nine times in a row, what are the odds it'll come up tails on the hundredth toss?" The answer's fifty-fifty, not ninety-nine to one, because there are only two sides on which a coin can fall.

All theories about fishing have a common flaw: they're theories and will remain in the realm of conjecture until we learn how to communicate with fish. No angler, regardless of the number of hours he spends experimenting, can say more than this: "Sometimes fish will take a fly dressed to a certain pattern, sometimes they'll ignore it." This may not be the most profound theory in the world, but it's the only one supported by the evidence at hand. I've yet to see an infallible fly or even a fly consistently productive more than 50 percent of the time. On the other hand, I've taken fish on a bare hook to which I'd wedged the head of a kitchen match, and on hooks to which I've tied a couple of strands of wool pulled out of my shirt-tail.

Exactly what combination of factors or conditions triggers a fish to strike an artificial fly is a secret and will remain so until we can talk to fish. Everything we now know about fish habits and response is based on empirical reasoning, which doesn't guarantee flawless conclusions.

This being the case, your opinions and theories about fly fishing, if based on honest study and observation, are as valid as the next angler's, and so are your interpretations of how a fly ought to be tied. That's the whole point of this approach to fly tying, and the above preamble on fly fishing and fishermen serves to illustrate it. Accept as a fact of life that all fly fishermen are opinionated, and that the deeper you get into tying the more opinions you'll hear from your angling friends. They'll tell you that fly A has hackle of the wrong shade, that fly B ought to have a tag as well as a tip, or vice versa, and that nobody in his right mind would substitute hairwings for feathers on fly C.

They're entitled to their opinions, and you're entitled to yours. If you were tying flies professionally, you'd have much less freedom to develop your own ideas than you do as an amateur. The professional fly tier is bound to traditional patterns, because if a customer orders a batch of Jock Scott salmon flies, the professional's obliged to use each of the twenty-three different pieces of material that are required in this fly's standard dressing. If you're tying the fly for your own use, you can leave something out or add something new — as long as it doesn't do damage to your conscience — and you'll probably find the fly just as effective.

A surprising number of excellent flies are the result of happenstance rather than study or observation. Legend credits the creation of the Professor to an English college instructor who arrived at a favorite trout stream, discovered he'd come out without his fly box and improvised a pattern by pulling threads out of his socks and using them to tie buttercup petals on hooks.

Reuben Cross, the famous Eastern master tier, didn't name his Cross Special after himself, as is popularly believed, but called it that because he "crossed" a Light Cahill with a Quill Gordon to see if the hybrid would take trout in upper New York streams. It did, and still does.

While I wasn't present on the night the famous Joe O'Donnell steelhead fly was created, I heard the story soon enough after the event from those who were, and since each of them told me privately and all their stories jibed, I'm ready to believe that the fly came to be tied the first time as a joke. The place was Joe's vanished and hence now-legendary cabin on the Klamath, where a half-dozen steelhead fishermen were consoling themselves after a fishless day with generous libations of ammis-gammis — the local name for spirituous beverages. Bert Wilson, whose friends called him Butch, remarked that they needed a new fly to change their luck the next day and was immediately bombarded with outlandish suggestions for its dressing. Getting out his fly-tying kit, Butch put together a new fly incorporating the wildest suggestions and proclaimed that his new creation was to be called the Joe O'Donnell. The fly proved a killer the next day and continues to take steelhead and, in smaller sizes, trout.

That successful flies were created jokingly or by accident doesn't lessen in any way the value of the patterns worked out during hours of painstaking study, observation, and deduction by such innovators as Pulham, Halford, LaBranche, Hewitt, Cross, Schwiebert, Wulff, Marinaro, and similar angling scholars. Nor do such creations lessen the nimbus of tradition that hovers over such ancient patterns as the Red Hackle or the Cowdung, of which Dame Juliana wrote nearly four centuries ago.

If there's a lesson to be learned from fly-fishing history, it is that the tier should do his best to honor the "standard" patterns but shouldn't let them become a strait jacket that forces him into a fixed, unalterable mold. Fly tying was born of experimenting, and experimenting knows no limits of calendars, decades, or even centuries.

Every fisherman who ties flies dreams of creating the irresistible pattern. Perhaps you're the one who will realize that still-elusive dream. The odds may be against it, but don't let that keep you from trying.

8

Tools and Materials

EQUIPPING YOURSELF FOR TYING flies is like setting up a workbench for any other craft: you can go all-out and load yourself down with tools that are useful but not essential, or you can confine yourself to the basics. A lot of veteran tiers who learned the art before many of today's accessories existed still get along with only four tools, so I'd put this as the minimum number with which you can function successfully.

Accessories are fine; I don't sneer at them or turn my back on them, even though I use very few myself. It comes down to what you learn when you're first beginning to acquire a skill; the tools you learn with come to be those you rely on because you're more at ease with them than with newer models. How many people do you know who learned to drive a car after automatic gearshifts became standard equipment, have never driven a car that didn't have one and look on the manual gearshift as a mysterious mechanism with which they don't even want to try to learn to cope?

TOOLS AND ACCESSORIES

Your essential needs, then, are four tools that you can buy for less than $20.00 from any tackle supply house. They are a vise, a pair of hackle pliers, a good pair of scissors, and a bodkin or stiletto, which you can make yourself by sticking the eye of a needle into a short length of dowel. The vise is your biggest investment, and please don't make the mistake so many novice tiers do, that is, tell yourself you'll get a cheap one to use until you decide whether you enjoy tying, and if you decide you do, then get a really good one. When you go this route you impose a handicap on yourself, because cheap, badly made vises make your fingers seem clumsier than they really are, and so you decide that tying's too difficult to learn, and give it up.

Look for a vise that has nicely tapered jaws that remain parallel to each other when they're closed. On better vises, a cammed lever or large knob opens and closes the jaws quickly, and there is an internal adjustment of the collet holding the jaws that allows them to be set at different gaps, to hold different sizes of hooks firmly but without damaging them. Some vises can be rotated without the fly being removed, to allow you to work on its underside. A good vise will run from $10.00 to $15.00, a deluxe vise about $20.00.

Hackle pliers are small, spring-loaded tweezers that open when squeezed together and close down to hold in their tips such delicate materials as the

All but a few of the tools pictured belong on the "necessary" list. Vises shown are, from left: Thompson Ultra, with tilting head; Thompson A, same as the Ultra but without tilt; Thompson B, which has a knob instead of a lever jaw-lock; Thompson Utility, with fine-tipped jaws that make it handy for small hooks; Thompson H, a light pressed-metal job chiefly useful for streamside tying; Thompson F, with heavy jaws to grip big bass and saltwater hooks. In left foreground, four types of bobbins; above, wax holder and hackle guards; center from bottom up, whip-finisher, materials, clips, bodkin; right from bottom, three types of hackle pliers, scissors, and nippers, hackle trimmer.

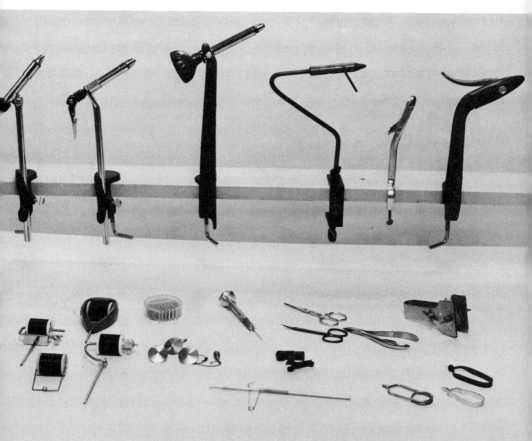

tip of a wispy feather or a tissue-thin piece of tinsel. There are several styles of these pliers, all work about equally well, and you'll probably come to feel most at home with whatever kind you get used to handling. They're not expensive, $1.00 to $1.50 a pair, so you can afford to discard a type you don't like and replace them with another type.

Scissors are the third tool. Cuticle scissors like those used by manicurists work very well, but if your fingers are at all large you'll find their loops uncomfortable. Special tying scissors with big finger loops are generally easier to use and cost very little more than the manicure scissors you'd pick up at the corner drugstore. If you feel like getting a second pair, get one with curved blades, as they're easier to work with in making tiny snipping cuts on delicate materials in tight places.

Scissors with large finger loops weren't available when I began tying flies, and I found lady-sized finger loops uncomfortable, so I transferred to fly tying the cuticle nippers — not scissors, but cutters that are a precision-made miniature version of electrician's wire cutters — that I'd used to cut off threads when building rods. These nippers are worthless for cutting things such as sections of wing fibers, but they're sturdy enough to cut hackle quills and can work closer to materials with greater safety than any other tool I've ever encountered. A lot of tiers use craft knives, such as the Exacto, which has very fine-tipped blades; some even use razor blades, but a slip of such a blade can undo a lot of painstaking work, and I feel safer with my needle-pointed nippers when cutting off materials.

A bodkin, sometimes called a stiletto, is the final essential tool. It's used for a number of jobs: separating feather fibers, holding materials temporarily in place, clearing hook eyes, fluffing out body materials by plucking at them, and so on. Bodkins are available in several styles and sizes, but I use a pin vise because it's so easy to replace a dulled point just by slipping in a fresh needle, or to change from a large to a small-sized needle when working on tiny hooks. You can make a bodkin by pushing the eye of a needle into a piece of dowel, or ask your dentist for an old probe, which makes a very fine bodkin indeed. Some tiers apply head cement with their bodkins, but I use cocktail toothpicks, which hold the liquid better and can be discarded when their tips get caked with lacquer.

Many tiers class a fifth tool as essential: a bobbin. These aren't like the bobbins on a sewing machine, so don't plan on heisting one from your wife. A tying bobbin holds a spool of thread and feeds the thread out through a small tube at controlled tension. There are many styles, and as is the case with so many special-purpose tools, choosing one is a matter of finding the style that feels most comfortable in your hand. All bobbins accomplish the same purpose, and since I learned to tie without using one, the only style with which I really feel comfortable is the simplest of all: a U-shaped piece of wire that simply keeps a spool of thread from unwinding if dropped and feeds thread through a simple loop in its top.

Tiers who learned with more sophisticated types of bobbin look on mine as primitive and makeshift, as perhaps it is, but I think I get a better feel of the thread tension when I handle it with my fingers, especially the more delicate threads. If you're new to handling thread, though, haven't done any rod wrapping or practiced other crafts that require its use, by all means learn to tie with a bobbin. Even my preference for the most primitive type doesn't blind me to the virtues of more elaborate models.

There are a lot of accessories you can add to your tying bench, and most of them are like bobbins: if you learn with them, you'll work with them, and they'll probably save you time and effort. But you can get along with the four tools just described, of which the most important is a good vise. I've known only one tier who worked without a vise, Mrs. E. C. Powell, wife of the famous rod builder. She'd been taught tying as a child by her father, who was a gillie on a Scottish estate, and it was fascinating to watch her work.

Holding the hook at its bend between the forefinger and thumb of her left hand, she kept that hand moving in a sort of weaving motion while guiding the thread and other materials into place with all five fingers of her right hand, somehow managing to keep thread and floss and herl and tinsel under complete control while forming the fly's body, then setting the wings and winding in the hackle without using pliers or tweezers. And her flies were not only beautifully balanced, they didn't come apart as did many others.

To return to the list of accessories you might well explore, some tiers find tweezers a help in handling, placing, and setting wings. Many use hackle guards to hold the barbules of feathers out of their way while finishing off a fly head. In the finishing tie, many tiers use a whip-finisher. Almost all tiers use material clips that snap onto a tying vise and hold loose ends of floss or dubbing or tinsel out of the working area, but I've found that two or three tiny bar magnets will do this job more efficiently, are easier to handle and don't get in my way as do the ends of standard clips.

There are devices that form neatly matched pairs of wings from quill feathers in one operation; there are trimmers that cut winging and hackling feathers into uniform shapes and sizes; half-hitch tools that can be used if you prefer this method of tying off heads; there are stands to hold materials neatly in order; special winging pliers to help you set and hold wings while tying them in; magnifying mirrors to be placed behind the vise so that you can see both sides of a fly at the same time; magnifiers and loupes of all kinds to help you see tiny hooks and fine materials more easily.

All these accessories perform very well the jobs for which they were designed, if you have trouble performing those operations with unassisted fingers. At one time or another, I've tried out most of them, but the habits formed when I learned tying always lead me back to using my fingers alone. After having watched a couple of hundred tiers at work, I've concluded that the best tool is practice. This is the only way to acquire that undefinable feel for materials, and I've noticed that the best tiers depend less on their eyes than they do on their fingers. At some point, after you've tied X number of flies, you'll find that if you overlap your thread or have a loose strand of herl in the five or six strands you're wrapping for a body, or a lump is beginning to form in your floss, your fingers will signal to you that these things are happening before you'll ever see them.

Your own needs will guide you to choosing the accessories that will be most useful. If after practicing you find an operation that defeats you, look around for an accessory that will help you perform it. If you don't need an accessory, don't buy it. It's as simple as that.

SUPPLIES

Short as the list of tying tools is, it's lengthy in comparison with the list of supplies — as distinguished from materials — that you will require. It consists of only two items: tier's wax and head cement. The wax is a composition of beeswax and rosin, and it's easier to buy than to make it, because you use relatively little. Wax comes in hard and soft forms, the soft wax being most useful when preparing dubbing, which is clipped fur or wool spun on a length of thread. Hard wax comes in cakes, and there's a holder for it that makes waxing a little easier. Soft wax comes in tins, and you can make a gadget that will help you wax thread with it. Get both kinds, you'll need both, and the wax costs very little.

Head cement or lacquer is used in a lot of operations: to tack down materials that are being tied in, such as a tail wisp or hackle butt; it's also used to coat nymph cases to make them hard and glossy, and to tack the fibers of a quill feather along the line of the quill to make it easier to cut them for winging; but the chief use of this cement is to coat the heads of flies and make them firm and glossy while at the same time protecting them from fraying. Head cement is usually a cellulose-acetone mixture, very similar to clear fingernail polish, which makes an adequate substitute. The cement can be thinned with acetone if it gets too gummy during use. There are also some acrylic-based head cements, which require special thinners. The cement comes in clear and black, but the clear is really all you need.

MATERIALS

Hooks

We now come to the materials list, at the head of which are hooks. As everyone who's done any fishing is aware, hooks come in an almost infinite variety of sizes, styles, and types; some are superior for flies, some useless. Among the photos are some actual-size pictures of the hooks most useful to the fly tier. However, since hook nomenclature is a part of many tying instructions, we do need to take at least a cursory look at hooks before going on to other materials.

Whatever the size or style or purpose of a hook, each part of it has its own name, these names being common to all hooks. The parts are the eye,

An assortment of Mustad hooks, shown in actual size, which are used for tying flies. They come in various sizes, with shanks of different lengths and thicknesses, and with either turned-up or turned-down eyes.

to which the line is attached; the shank, or straight section extending back from the eye; the bend, which begins at the end of the shank and curves to a spot in line with the rearmost tip of the barb; and the point, which is the entire area of the barb. The distance between the shank and the point is called the gap, and the space from the rearmost curve of the bend to a line drawn between point and shank is called the throat.

Hook sizes are expressed in terms of the width of the gap and are given in numbers graduating both up and down from one. Hooks below a certain size are indicated by even numbers that increase as the hook size diminishes, #2, #4, #6, and so on down to #28, which is the smallest hook made. The larger sizes are indicated by numbers in regular sequence followed by /0. Thus, hooks numbered 1/0, 2/0, 3/0, and so on increase in size up to 20/0, the largest hook made in standard patterns. There are bigger hooks, but these are measured in inches of gap width.

Extralong shanks are designated by numbers in sequence from 1 to 4 followed by X, which indicate that the shank length is normally that of a hook that number of sizes larger. Thus, a hook described as #8 1X has a shank as long as that of a #6 hook, a #8 2X has a shank as long as that of a #4 hook, and so on. Long-shanked hooks are used principally for tying streamer flies and large wet flies.

There are also hooks having shorter than normal shanks, but these are usually called by the name "spider hooks," describing the special kind of fly tied on them.

There are three different diameters of wire used in hooks designed for fly fishing, and in practice all hooks that are not described as being of "fine" or "stout" wire are understood to be of standard-diameter wire. This is .035 (35 thousandths of an inch) in #1 hooks and goes down to .016 in the #28 size. "Fine" or "light" wire is .028 in #1 hooks and goes down to .014 in the #28 size. The diameter of "stout" or "heavy" wire hooks begins at .042 in #1 size and drops to .019 in the #10 size, which is the smallest hook made with heavy wire. Slight as these variations might appear, the difference between the floating ability of a dry fly tied on fine and standard hooks is noticeable, as is the difference in sinking quality of a wet fly tied on standard and stout hooks.

Most flies are tied on hooks having turned-down eyes, through many tiers favor turned-up eyes for nymphs and wet flies. Large flies such as bucktails and streamers designed to be fished behind a spinner are customarily tied on ringed eye hooks, which are in a line with the shank. The designation for turned-up eye hooks is TUE, that for turned-down eye hooks is TDE.

While there are twenty-five or thirty different kinds of hook bends, we need be concerned with only three: round, sproat, and Limerick. The round bend is just what its name implies, an arc of a circle. Mustad and Alcock, the leading hook manufacturers, have trade names for their round-bend hooks; Mustad's is called the Viking, Alcock's the Model Perfect. The sproat and Limerick bends are shaped in an arc that is the apex of an oval, with the point extending from the center of the apex. The two shapes are very much alike, their chief difference being that the oval bend of a Limerick hook is slightly sharper than that of a sproat. There is a salmon-fly hook called the Dublin Point Limerick that has a slightly straighter eye than the standard version; it also has a looped turned-up eye and is finished in japanned black, the traditional finish for salmon-fly hooks.

Manufacturers give their hooks a "quality number," which has nothing to do with the intrinsic quality of the hook but describes the type of steel, the tempering — how flexible or brittle the wire is — and whether the hook wire is round or forged into a rectangle. More important to you is the fact that this number is also a sort of shorthand that includes all the hook's specifications: wire weight, eye type, bend, length. It's not only a convenience to the dealer and manufacturer, but to you as a buyer. It's much easier to tell your dealer that you want a box of "Mustad 7948A #8" than it would be to list all the hook's features covered by the quality number.

Just what hooks you decide to use is up to you and will depend to a very large extent on the flies you'll be tying. For the average tier's bench, I'd say standard hooks in sizes #14 through #8 in fine wire for dry flies, sizes up to #6 in heavy wire for wets, and whatever long-shanked hooks you might need for bucktails and streamers. But hook selection is pretty much a personal matter. I long ago began putting most of my flies on round-bend hooks, using the longer shanked Limericks for streamers. Except for nymphs and midges, I tie just about everything on TDE hooks.

Silk, wool, fur, and feathers

Finally, now, we've arrived at the stage of looking at silk and wool, fur and feathers. Because materials are so often interchanged in function when flies are being tied, it's just about impossible to classify every material by its use. About the best we can do is to start at the foundation and work up.

Thread is the foundation of all flies. It was once called "tying silk," perhaps because male tiers hesitated to use a word like "thread" that had feminine connotations. The fact that tying thread was initially made from silk certainly also had something to do with the name. Today, nylon is the material from which tying thread is most commonly made, though nymph specialists swear by a gauzy extrafine silk for the creations they dress on tiny hooks. For general use, size 000 is about right, though when dressing big streamers I like the heavier 00 and A, and go on up to the big threads, D and E, for saltwater flies.

For tying on small hooks, there is an extruded nylon thread called Monocord, which is much easier to use than 000000 regular thread, and which can be used on the very tiny hooks to form bodies and for ribbing. All tying threads come in several colors, though you will find black the most useful; white is handy if you're dubbing fur of a very light hue and don't want a black thread to show through the fur. Only a few flies require colored heads, which is about the only reason I can see for using a thread other than black for general-purpose tying.

Color is king, however, when you move on to other materials. The body materials you'll use most often are floss, wool, and dubbing, the latter being fur or wool spun on tying thread. Floss is composed of tiny filaments that are either untwisted or very lightly twisted into threadlike form. It is designed to overlap smoothly on a hook. Silk is the finest floss material, nylon is almost as good, but rayon should be avoided; it is brittle in tiny diameters and breaks and fuzzes up on hooks. Floss comes in a huge color range; the most useful colors are cream, yellow, tan, brown, light and dark blue, light and dark green, olive, scarlet, orange, and black. A few patterns call for claret, a few for white.

There is a special floss made of synthetic fibers that is used in conjunction with a solvent that fuses the fibers into a unified mass. The fusing process is not instantaneous, so while the floss is reacting to the solvent you can squeeze or otherwise form a fly body built with this material. This is especially useful in nymph tying.

Wool for fly tying is generally smaller in diameter and of a harder twist than knitting wool. Crewel yarn is especially useful, and all wool can be divided into its individual strands for use on small hooks. The regular diameter of fly-tying wool is more useful for big flies, and the color range you'll need corresponds to floss.

In the late 1960s, fly tiers discovered that polypropylene fiber has a specific gravity less than that of water. This, of course, means that the material will float and makes possible the dressing of flies that don't need to be held on the water's surface by the combined effects of a number of hackle tips. Polypropylene, often called "poly-yarn," is carried by many tackle suppliers either as a spun yarn or in the form of loose fibers that can be spun onto tying thread like any other dubbing material.

Chenille is another important body material; it is made by intertwining short strands of very fine fibers between two strands of thread. It is very easy to use and comes in four diameters numbered from 2 to 5, of which the #3 and #5 sizes are the most useful. Its colors are in the same range as those of floss and wool.

Herl and quill are other useful body materials, the quill being often secured by stripping the fuzz from herl. Peacock herl comes from the strips radiating from the big center quill of a peacock's tail feathers and from the bird's sword. In color, peacock herl ranges from a brilliant blue or blue-green in the sword to a greenish bronze in the tail, and it has a naturally iridescent quality that seems fatally attractive to fish. Peacock herl is used not only for fly bodies but also as ribbing, shouldering, tags, tails, butt joints, topping, and as legs or feelers in nymphs. It can be bought as full quills or stripped and sewn on a thread. Ostrich herl comes from the main fiber feathers and is naturally white to a creamy tan, but is also dyed to many other shades.

Quills come from many sources: porcupines, feathers, herl, and coarse-haired animals. The fibers of large-feathered birds such as the condor provide quills, and so does herl when stripped of its fibers. Akin to quill, but used in only a few fly patterns, is raffia. Straw is also called for, dyed or natural, in some patterns.

Tinsel, gold- or silver-finished, is used for ribbing, but a number of flies have all-silver or all-gold bodies. Tinsel comes in several widths, and the most popular type now is Mylar, which is gold-colored on one side, silver on the other. Mylar does not tarnish as does metallic tinsel, but it cannot be had in the fine wire sizes of the metallic type. You can get by very well with a spool each of wide, medium, and fine Mylar tinsel plus a spool of gold and silver wire.

Fur plays several different roles in fly tying. It is used as a body material, being cut into short lengths and spun or rolled onto waxed tying thread; this is called "dubbing," and the process will be detailed later. The furs most often used in dubbing are muskrat, fox, rabbit or hare, Australian opossum, beaver, seal, mole, and mink. You can get by quite well with muskrat, light and dark fox, hare, and one of the dark furs such as seal, beaver, or otter.

A distinction should be made here between fur and hair. Fur is soft and generally used only as a body material; hair in the fly tier's vocabulary means coarse fibers such as deer, bear, moose, calf-tail (impala), and antelope. Polar bear hair, once a very popular hair, is no longer available and has been replaced by a synthetic. Hair is used for winging flies, for tails, sometimes for throat hackle. Moose mane, a coarse, crinkly hair, is often used like quill to form bodies. Deer hair, which, like the hair of other antlered animals such as elk and antelope, is hollow, can be tied on a hook so that it flares out; it is then clipped to form a body for a large fly. Almost all hair can be bought in small quantities, attached to the skin of the animal. Many hairs are dyed. Your hair assortment should include natural and dyed deerhair, natural antelope, a grey and brown squirrel tail, black bear, a natural white hair, and some synthetic polar bear hair.

Keep your hunting friends in mind as a potential source of hair and fur, and don't overlook taxidermy shops. Animals being mounted often yield scraps of hair-covered skin when being trimmed to fit the mounting form, and these scraps provide enough material for a lot of flies.

Feathers used in fly tying come from almost every kind of bird that flies or walks and have many applications. Basically, there are three types of feathers: quills, which come from the wings, tail, and back; body feathers, from the breast and flanks; and hackle, from the neck and saddle – what we'd call hips in a human. Most fly tiers like to use natural, undyed feathers if possible, as even the most careful and expert dye job removes a certain amount of the sheen or gloss that characterizes natural feathers. However, there is a chronic scarcity of some shades of natural feathers, and this drives the prices of the scarce items up to the point where most of us settle for a well-dyed feather in many cases.

Wings for flies are formed from sections of fibers cut from the wing, tail, and back quills; from tips of hackle; from the tips of body feathers; and in a few instances from crest or neck plumage. Hackle is formed from the tiny, almost webless feathers of fowl necks, and from the longer, limper feathers of their saddles. Neck hackle is needed for dry flies, saddle hackle for wet flies. The best neck hackle comes from gamecocks or gamecock cross-breeds, and from the necks of tough old roosters. You can buy hackle as whole or half-necks, as well as strung on threads in uniform sizes, bunched in uniform sizes, in packets either of uniform sizes or unsized. Unless you tie a huge number of flies, a neck or half-neck is an oversupply, since the hackles will get brittle with age before you use all of them. A ½-ounce packet will contain 250 to 300 feathers and is probably your best buy. Brown, grizzly, ginger, black, cream or white, dun blue-grey, olive, scarlet, badger, and furnace (also called coch-y-bondhu) are the hackles you will use most often.

Plumage, or fancy feathers, come from ringneck and silver pheasants, grouse, partridge, guinea hens, marabou storks, turkeys, geese, and most ducks. Some feathers called for in old fly patterns come from birds that are now protected species or that world events have removed from the plumage market. Dyed imitations are in most cases available. Perhaps the most-missed fowl is the jungle cock, whose body plumage was once widely used in feathering flies, and whose neck yielded short, thin, reddish orange and black feathers with creamy spots which came to be called "jungle-cock eyes" and are called for in many patterns. These feathers were always in short supply, for jungle cocks were never domesticated, but were taken by native hunters in the Southeast Asian jungles; wars did away with the birds and the hunters as well. Some suppliers offer plastic "eyes," and a few have hand-painted feathers that can be substituted.

Laying in a stock of fancy feathers is a long-term project; your best bet is to buy an assortment such as is offered by many suppliers, then replenish with individual feathers those you find you use most often. A few kinds that you will need with fair consistency are teal breast, barred wood duck, guinea fowl, and pheasant tippet and crest. These are the items that recur most often in pattern lists.

There are a few types of material that fall into the category of odd bits and pieces: lead wire to weight hooks if you tie big wet flies for use in fast water; porcupine quill for nymph legs; moose mane for feelers; split brass globes to make heads for Optic series flies; rubber body material if you tie bugs; hump-shank hooks and corks for bass bugs and poppers. In time, you'll acquire these and other small items that you use only occasionally.

Viewed as a whole, the variety and quantity of fly-tying materials is enough to stagger, perhaps to dismay, newcomers to the art, and to give them dire visions of having to invest a small fortune in order even to begin. It really isn't that daunting. The thing to do is to buy in small quantities, and a kit that offers a variety of materials is the best way to go. You won't get large quantities of any single item in a kit, but perhaps that's better than overbuying on something you'll use only occasionally. You can always fill in the gaps by getting the individual items that the kit didn't provide in sufficient quantity.

Most fly-tying materials aren't expensive in the amounts you need to produce quite a substantial number of flies, and between half and two-thirds of the items used aren't perishable. Some things, such as feathers, grow brittle and lackluster with age, but others, such as wool and floss, stay usable almost indefinitely; I've got floss and wool and fur and a few other things in my kit that are twenty or more years old and seem to improve with age, like a fine wine.

But judge your outlay by some prices current at this writing: chenille 5¢ to 6¢ a yard; floss about ½¢ a yard; tinsels 4¢ a yard; loose neck hackle in packets, 40¢ to 50¢ for 100 to 150 selected feathers; matched pairs of wing quills, from 10¢ to 75¢ or $1.00, depending on the bird's rarity; and so on down the list. If you buy carefully in small quantities you can stock a very respectable cabinet for $10.00 or so. Remember, an inch of body material, a couple of feathers, and a smidge of this or that is all a fly requires. Small quantities last a long time.

Finally, there's the problem of where you're going to keep all that material between tying sessions. A lot of my friends like cigar boxes, reserving each box for a separate material, or putting a cardboard divider in a box to provide two, three, or four separate compartments. Some use the little metal small-parts cabinets that sell for around $5.00. Others do as I did years ago: build a frame to fit around several kitchen-drawer divided cutlery trays so that these trays become compartmented drawers. It really doesn't make much difference what form your storage system or cabinet takes as long as it fits your needs.

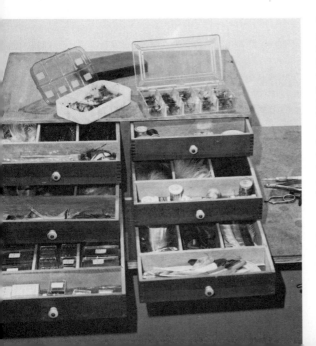

This may not be a typical tier's cabinet, but it's mine, and I've used it so many years I'm too lazy to change. Besides that, it works. The retreaded kitchen cutlery trays fitted with drawer-pulls have four compartments; the top left drawer holds body feathers and herl, the middle drawer hackle, the bottom drawer hooks. From top right the drawers hold floss, wool, chenille, and thread; hair and tinsel; winging quills. Tools and bits and pieces of partly used material go into the front compartments that run the width of the trays. Like every tier's cabinet I've ever seen, it's always too full.

However, you do need some kind of organized method to keep hackle and quills and herl and floss and tinsel and so on separated so that you can reach for the things you want to use without rummaging through a tangled skein of materials. Ideally, the system you arrive at will include some kind of containers for moth-prone materials such as wool, feathers, and fur that can be tightly sealed when you're not going to be doing any tying for an extended period. And, before sealing your containers, be sure to sprinkle in a few moth crystals or give them a whiff of antimoth spray.

Fly tying's essentially a tabletop operation, so a working area shouldn't present any difficulties. Set aside a corner of your workbench if it's arranged for sit-down working, or use a card table in the living room, or get a big square of plywood that you can put on your wife's best table to clamp your vise on. A lot of wives are unsympathetic to fly-tying husbands who clamp their vises on dining tables.

Now that we're all set in the departments of tools and materials, we can finally get around to tying some flies.

9

General Tying Procedures

As we've already learned, the first fishing fly noted in written history was of very simple construction: a wrap of wool and a pair of feathers. This remained the situation until well into the 19th century; flies generally consisted of only wings, body, and perhaps a tail. All flies were fished underwater until about the 1830s or 1840s, though late in the 1700s a few daring innovators were suggesting that it might be possible to take fish on a floating fly. Generally, though, tiers before the 1850s were more concerned with imitating a drowned insect than a live one floating on the water. This changed as anglers in increasing numbers responded to the dry fly's challenge, and as time went on, patterns began to become more and more complex.

Fly tying—dressing is the precise word but is used less often now than formerly—was for many years a sort of family affair. This was partly due to the British life-style, for Britain was the cradle of fly fishing. Open waters were rare in the little island kingdom, where fishing was a leisure-class sport. It was the custom for the owners of the great castles and manors to invite friends to fish, and to provide them with all the necessary tackle. The job of looking after the tackle was delegated to a gillie—ghillie, in Scotland—who, under the supervision of the head gamekeeper, not only maintained the rods and lines but provided the bait, including his own tied flies, and acted as a guide and helper at streamside. It's interesting to note that during this period an angler hooked and played a fish until it was ready to be landed, then handed the rod to the gillie, who brought the fish in to net.

Since the son of any family dependent on the castle was automatically expected to step into his father's shoes, the art of tying flies was handed down from father to son. Younger sons leaving the estates to make their own way kept the secrets learned from their fathers and passed them on to their sons in turn. Individual tiers guarded their secrets jealously, some even hinting darkly that their flies were more effective because sorcery or witchcraft played a part in preparing the materials used in their tying.

Today, of course, the reverse is true; tiers are generous in sharing discoveries with their fellow anglers.

ANATOMY OF A FLY

As years rolled on, and fly patterns grew in complexity, it became necessary to give names to the various parts of a fly's anatomy, names that would be understood universally. Technically, there are now sixteen parts in a fly dressing that have their own names, but few patterns include all these variations. In recent years the trend has been away from elaborately dressed flies; they are even beginning to fade from the salmon fly-fishing scene, which is the branch of fly fishing in which heavily dressed flies traditionally play the most prominent part.

If you're going to be able to reproduce a fly you've never seen, guided only by a description of its pattern, you need to know all the traditional parts of a fly's anatomy. In the accompanying picture these are shown in four groups, tail section, body section, wing section, and head section. Bear in mind as you look at the pictures that the materials shown aren't necessarily tied on the hook in the sequence these groupings might indicate. More about this later on; right now let's undertake a brief anatomical examination.

A fly's tail section may be composed of four parts; from the bend of the hook to the shank, these are the tip, the tag, the tail, and the tail topping. The last is seldom seen in modern dressing. The tip is most often of tinsel or floss; these materials are also the ones most used in the tag. The tail may be a wisp of hackle fibers, the tip of a hackle feather, some fibers from a body feather or a wing quill, a short piece of wool or some short lengths of herl, or fibers from a fancy feather such as the tippets from a golden pheasant neck or crest. If topping is used in the tail section it may be of almost any material.

Parts of a Fly

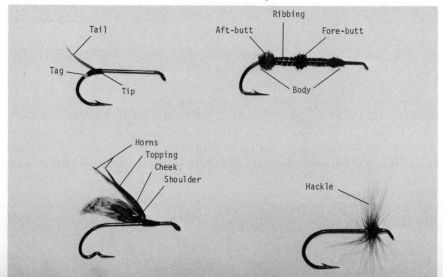

In most cases, a fly's body is made from only one kind of material: floss, wool, chenille, quill, herl, or dubbing; less often it may be of tinsel, raffia, or some other material. Some fly patterns have divided bodies, in which case the terms "fore" and "aft" are used to designate the front and back sections respectively. A divided body may be made of two different kinds of material, or it may be broken by a band in the center, which is called a joint or center joint; if additional material such as hackle is used, it is known as a trailer or trailers. Small sections of material at either end are called butts, and it is understood that if only one butt is used it will be at the back of the body and will have no additional description, but if a butt is also added at the front of the body, the butts are referred to as the fore-butt and aft-butt. Ribbing is a spiral of material that usually runs the length of the body.

There are several different types of wings, which will be covered later; here, we're concerned only with the names of parts associated with the wing section. If wings of contrasting colors or materials are used, they become the under and upper wings. A different material outside, and shorter than, the wing is a shoulder, a still shorter piece of material is a cheek, and an even shorter piece is an eye. The last is the most common, and few flies have all four pieces. Long, thin pieces of material tied outside and along the wings are called strips; similar pieces above the wing are called topping, and any material above the topping is called horns.

Just ahead of the wing are feather wisps called hackle. Dry-fly hackle is full and bushy and sometimes surrounds the wings. Wet-fly hackle is long and wispy and is almost always confined to the area ahead of the wings. Another type of wet-fly hackle is made from wisps of feathers or hair and tied under the throat, like a long beard; it is called throat hackle, and the type is generally specified in the pattern. If layers of hackle are used at the throat, they will be listed as "under" or "over"; thus "red over green over blue" would mean that the topmost layer would be red, the middle layer green, the bottom layer blue. Wrapped hackle may be layered or mixed, and mixed hackle comes under the same designation as that applied to throat hackle, "over" or "under." However, when hackle is to be tied in layers on a wrapped-hackle fly, the front layer is known as the face.

Finally, the fly is finished off with the head, which is made by wrapping the portion of the shank between hackle and eye with layers of thread. It is applied symmetrically, tied off, the excess trimmed, and the thread then coated with head lacquer. This is not shown in the pictures, but will be detailed later.

It's an almost universal custom when writing a fly pattern to list the materials in the order in which they are tied in during the fly's construction, thus: tip, tag, tail, topping, ribbing, body with any sections or divisions it might have, wings, and hackle. A tier can then follow the written description in constructing the fly without having to backtrack and add material in a clumsy manner.

PREPARATION OF MATERIALS

Much of the material used in fly tying is ready to use as purchased, but some materials must be prepared or treated before they go onto the hook. The procedures followed in treating these materials are the same, whether you're tying wet or dry flies, bass bugs, bucktails, tiny nymphs, or giant flies for use in saltwater. Let's take up these common procedures now and then look at the several steps you will take when tying any fly. Then, we can explore the special steps involved in tying different kinds of flies.

Your foundation of thread must be made ready by waxing the thread. Some tiers buy prewaxed thread, others wax an entire spool at once. This is fine if you're tying flies often and in large numbers, but I like to work with freshly waxed thread, especially when using a soft wax, because I think it makes tying easier. There's a rough, lumpy feel to thread that's been waxed for a long time. It takes only a couple of minutes to pull 10 feet of thread through a cake of wax, or to push the thread into a tin of soft wax and pull it through. To keep my fingers clean I bend a shallow upside-down U in one end of a straightened out paper clip and use the bent tip to hold the thread in the wax as I pull it through.

Waxing with cake or solid wax is faster and neater with the help of a holder.

Make your own holder to use with soft wax by bending a paper clip, as shown, with which to push the thread down into the wax.

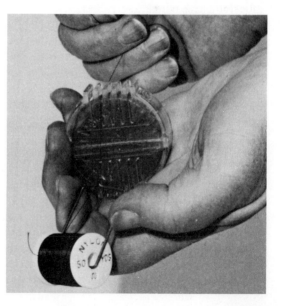

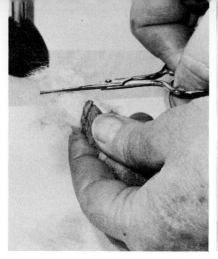
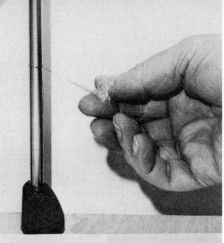

To prepare dubbing on its own thread, start by cutting fur and combing out the long guard hairs from the underbody fur.

After heavily waxing a length of tying thread, anchor it with a loop to the base of your vise (above right). Pick up a small tuft of fur and spin it on the thread with your fingers, always turning the fur in the same direction. The size of the hooks you'll use it on governs the diameter of your fur "rope," and shank length the quantity needed.

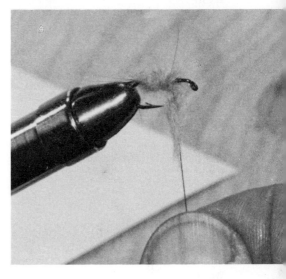

After dubbing enough for a fly body, wrap it on the hook (right). If you misjudge the amount needed you can always pull off the excess or add a bit more.

Spinning fur or wool on thread to wrap into a body, the step called dubbing, can be done before you begin tying dubbed bodies, or you can dub the fur on the thread you're tying with at the point in your work when you're ready for it. You do the same thing whichever time you choose. First your fur or wool or other body material must be prepared. Hold the material over a clean sheet of paper and clip off the quantity you'll need, then pick up the separate small pieces of fur or wool and clip them into shorter pieces. Pull the matted fur apart between your fingertips as you work. Next, loop a piece of well-waxed thread over the column of your vise, and with the thread held taut, roll small pinches of clipped fur onto the thread. Roll in only one direction, and keep pushing the fur along the thread to fill bare spots, until you've formed a uniformly thick covering on the thread. If you're working in the vise, hold the tying thread tight when you're ready to form the body, have the fur clipped and prepared, and simply dub on enough to form the fly's body.

Like most of the operations you'll perform in tying, making dubbing is a simple job that requires very little time. However, if you must meter the hours you can put in working on flies, or don't feel like keeping a supply of the raw materials needed, you can buy ready-made dubbing that's satisfactory for all but the very smallest sizes of flies. It's used like any other thread-type material.

While several kinds of quills are used in making quill bodies, you'll probably be working with the quill from peacock herl more than any other, since it's inexpensive, versatile, and easy to prepare. There are two methods of stripping the tiny, fuzzy fibers from the herl; one is used if you want natural-colored herl, the other involves bleaching the herl so that the quill can be colored. To dry-strip herl, work on a clean sheet of paper or cardboard. Lay the quill out straight, hold it down with a finger pressed to

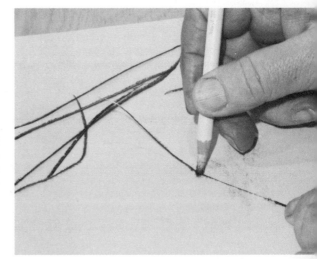

Strip herl on a clean sheet of paper, using a very soft eraser. Hold the herl by the tip and rub with the eraser toward the butt.

its tip, and run an eraser along the quill toward the base. Many erasers are too hard to do this job; the best I've found is a pencil-type eraser made by Eberhard Faber; its number is 1966. A slightly firmer eraser, #1507, made by the same firm, works better on larger quills.

If you want bleached quill, the bleaching process removes the fibers at the time they're bleached. Prepare the bleach bath of any standard wash-day bleach such as Clorox, using about 1 teaspoon of bleach to 2 table-spoons of cold water. Pour the bleach over the quills in a plate or large saucer and take them out at once when they turn white. The fuzz will shed off at this point. The effects of the bleach must be neutralized by putting the quills immediately into a solution made by dissolving 1 teaspoon of baking soda in 1 cup of cold water. Let the quills stay in the neutralizing bath for about five minutes.

Unless bleached herl quill is used wet, it has a tendency to get brittle and split or break when wrapped on a hook. You can prepare a quantity of herl quill in advance and overcome its brittleness, which increases as the bleached quills age in storage, by soaking the bleached and neutralized quills in a diluted solution of photographic print flattener such as Pakosol or Kodak Print Flattener. Use about 10 drops of the concentrated solution in 1 cup of water. Or you can make your own preservative bath by mixing 1/4 teaspoon of isopropyl alcohol (91% strength) with 1 tablespoon of glycerine, then stirring this into 1 pint of lukewarm water. The mixture keeps well in a stoppered bottle but may throw down a deposit in time; it does not harm the solution, just strain to clear it. Quills that have been bleached will stay fresh and flexible for six to eight months after being soaked for about ten minutes in any of the solutions mentioned here.

Although Mylar has just about replaced metal as a tinsel, metal wire tinsel is still used for very tiny flies that need a gold or silver ribbing, since Mylar is not made in small enough dimensions. Even the best metal tinsel will tarnish with age, in use or in storage, and in the days when all tinsel was metal, tiers kept tarnish from spoiling their stock of tinsel by pulling it through their fingertips after moistening one fingertip with a drop of head lacquer. The cement dries instantly and will keep metallic tinsel tarnish-free.

There are several devices available for forming wing sections from quills. Most of them use a coarse-toothed, sawlike comb that fits into a clamp that holds the feather and marks off evenly spaced sections along the center quill. I've found it's as easy and takes less time simply to separate the fibers with the point of a bodkin when making fiber feather wings.

There are also several devices that can be used to trim hackle that is too wide for the size of flies on which you want to use it. These are usually a U-shaped handle with a pair of adjustable parallel blades that are pressed down on the feather while it rests on a piece of cardboard. Again, it's just as easy to select the right width of hackle to start with; you'll probably spend no more time looking than you would in adjusting the trimmer and cutting the feathers. Some of these machines are advertised as being able to convert wet-fly hackle into the more costly kind suitable for dry flies, but the key to dry-fly hackle isn't its width, but the absence of webbing from the feathers and the stiffness of their fibers. Wet-fly hackle just doesn't have these qualities, and there's nothing you can do about it.

Some tiers save working time by preparing in advance the hackle they plan to use during a tying session. All hackle needs to be stripped and stroked before it's tied in; the fuzzy bottom webbing must be removed by holding the quill of the feather and pulling the fuzz off with even tension in the direction of the feather's butt. Then, the feather is held by its tip, and the fibers are gently stroked against the grain to separate them and cause them to stand out at right angles to the quill. I'm not sure how much actual time is saved by doing this in advance, but it does avoid interrupting the tying while you search for the hackle for each fly.

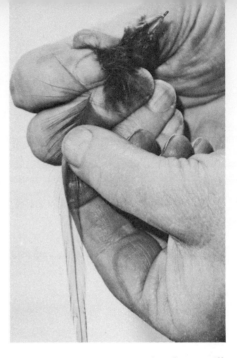

To prepare hackle for tying in, hold a feather firmly by the quill and strip off the webby, downy bottom fibers by pulling them gently but firmly toward the butt of the quill. Then, hold the feather by its tip and stroke it between thumb and forefinger against the grain to separate the fibers and cause them to stand out at right angles from the quill.

There are a few more advance preparations you can make, but we'll cover these later in the description of the actual tying process.

THE TYING PROCESS

Let's look now at the steps in tying that are common to all kinds of flies, regardless of size or type. In the accompanying pictures, for the sake of simplification the various steps are shown on hooks bare of any material except that which is involved in the stage in question, so use your imagination a bit to visualize how these steps must be handled when you get to them in the course of putting a fly together.

To start the thread on the hook, lay its loose end along the shank and overwrap this end with several turns. While the turns are widely spaced in the photo, they should actually be close together. When you've made a half-dozen tight turns over the thread-end, clip if off close to the point at which the overwrapping ends. Continue wrapping back along the shank toward the bend until you reach the spot where the first piece of material is to be tied in. Keep your foundation wrap tight and smooth, the thread touching each preceding turn.

Usually the tip or tag will go on the fly first, and this is generally tinsel. Cut a strip of tinsel, choosing a width suitable for the size of hook being used. The hook pictured is a #2 Mustad 7948A, chosen because it's big enough to be seen clearly; for this same reason a 00 white thread is being used. The hook size calls for a strip of medium-width tinsel, which should be brought up between thread and hook so that a single turn of the thread will lock the strip in place. Make a second turn of the thread toward the bend of the hook and clip off the excess end of the tinsel.

Tying in the Tip

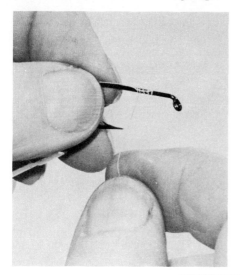

1. Start your tying thread on the hook by laying the free end along the hook shank and looping the thread around the hook over the thread. After five or six turns, clip off the loose end. The turns in the picture are spaced widely to show the detail; you'd actually wrap each turn to touch the one made ahead of it.

2. Continue wrapping along the shank until you reach the spot above the barb where you'll tie in the first materials.

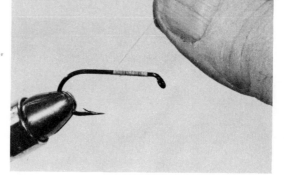

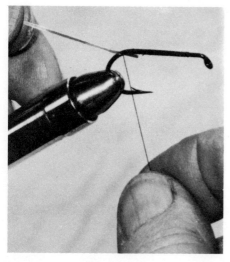

3. To start tinsel on the hook, hold the tip of the piece being tied on at a slight angle to the hook shank and bring the thread up over the shank, around the tinsel. Make two or three turns with the thread and clip off the end of the tinsel (continued).

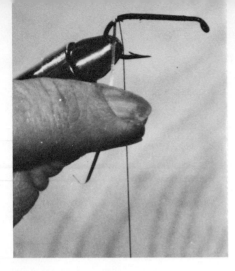

4. Keeping the flat side of the tinsel parallel to the hook, spiral it around the shank in smooth, tight turns. The space between each turn should be a tiny bit less than the width of the tinsel. For a tag, as shown here, make two or three wraps.

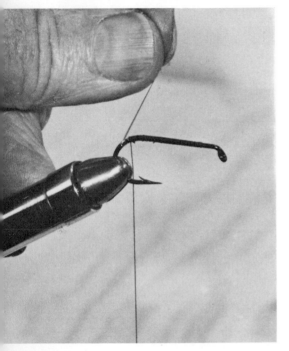

5. When you begin backwrapping, hold the tinsel angled forward as illustrated and fill the gaps left between turns. If you're tying a fly with a tinsel body, tie in the tinsel at the front of the hook, wrap back in an open spiral, then forward to fill the spaces.

6. End your backwrap when tinsel meets thread, bring the thread up, over, and around the hook and tinsel, then make a safety turn with the thread to anchor the tinsel; some tiers add a drop of head cement.

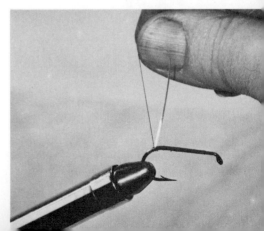

Wrap the tinsel down along the bend in two turns spaced about half the width of the tinsel apart. Then angle the tinsel in the opposite direction and wind up the hook, covering the spaces left by the down-wrap. When you reach the point where the tinsel was tied in, bring the thread across the tinsel with one hand while keeping tension on the strip with the other. Two turns of the thread are enough to keep the tinsel in place. Pull the thread across the top of the hook with one hand, clip the tinsel strip as close as possible with the other. Many tiers put a small drop of head lacquer on the tied-off thread as an extra precaution, and if the tinsel hasn't been coated and is metallic rather than Mylar, it should be coated with lacquer now.

Next comes the tail. Strip the unmarked fibers from a pheasant tippet and use the bodkin to separate enough marked fibers to form a tail of a size suited to the hook. Trim the separated fibers close to the quill and, without letting go of them, roll them gently between thumb and finger into a compact cylinder. Still without letting go of the feather wisp, place it over the hook; the tail should be equal in length to the hook shank, so hold the wisp over the hook so that the portion beyond the point where the tying thread passes is long enough.

Bring the tying thread up over the tippet wisp in a loop; well-waxed thread is stiff enough so that you can control it in this operation. Tighten the thread firmly and make two wraps to anchor the tippet. Then trim off the excess fibers in front of the tie-in point. If the fly pattern had called for a tip and a tag, the extra material would have been inserted between tinsel and feathers, and attached to the hook just like the tinsel.

Basically, the method of tying in body material such as floss or wool or quill is the same as that used in tying in the tinsel. If wool or floss is used, it's a good idea to moisten the end of the strip and roll it between thumb and forefinger to avoid fuzzing when it takes the pressure of the tying thread. Hold the body material below the hook and at a slight angle across the shank, then bring the thread up and over to tie in the material. In the case illustrated, it's floss, and the hook is the same size as that used in the preceding pictures.

When the floss has been tied in and the excess trimmed, carry your tying thread forward along the shank in wide spirals until it reaches the point where the body will end. Then begin wrapping the body material forward on the shank. When the body material is wrapped to the point at which the thread is stopped, begin wrapping the floss back along the shank, taking double or even triple turns to form a neatly tapering body. On reaching your starting point at the end of the shank, wrap forward once more, again making double or triple turns as needed in the center section to give the body a satisfactory taper. Tie off the body material just as the tinsel was tied off. This is the method used to form a fly body from wool, chenille, floss, or any other material that is prestranded.

Tying in the Tail

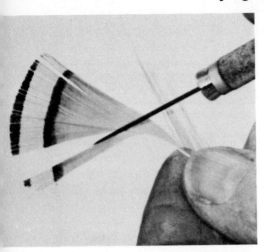

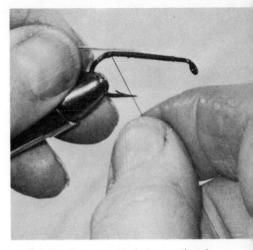

1. For a pheasent-tippet tail, use the bodkin to divide a wisp of fibers by pushing the point in at the quill and running it out between the fibers to the edge. Once you've trimmed the fibers, don't let go.

2. Roll the fibers gently between thumb and forefinger to form them into a neat, small cylinder and hold them over the hook with the wisp at the point where it will be tied in.

3. Bring the thread up and over the feather wisp and hook without touching or putting any pressure on the wisp. Tighten the loop only after it's been brought under the hook shank.

4. As it closes on the wisp, the thread will pull the fibers straight down on the shank without causing them to separate. Take two turns to tie in and clip the wisp in front of the thread.

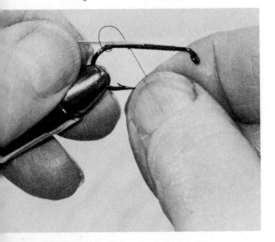

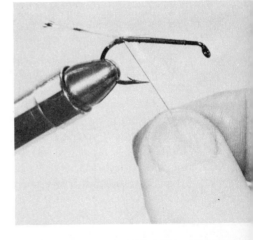

Tying in the Floss

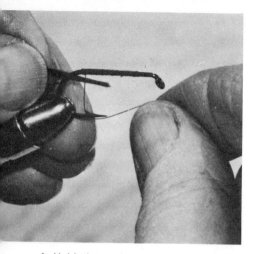

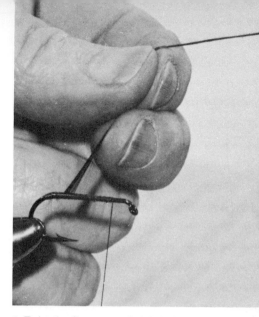

1. Hold the moistened end parallel to and just below the hook shank and bring the thread up over floss and hook. Tighten the thread as you pull it back of the hook, take an anchoring turn, and clip excess floss. Wrap the thread forward to where the body will end.

2. Twist the floss very slightly before you start to wrap, or it will splay out as it's doing in the picture. If this happens, use a fingertip pressed gently against the floss to stop the splaying until you've wrapped past the point where it began to spread.

3. At the point where the fly body will end, begin wrapping the floss back along the shank. Make extra turns at the forepart to start giving the body its taper. After back-wrapping to the tail, wrap forward again.

4. Continue to wrap to the point where the body ends, cross the thread over the floss and take two turns of thread to anchor the floss to the hook, then clip the floss.

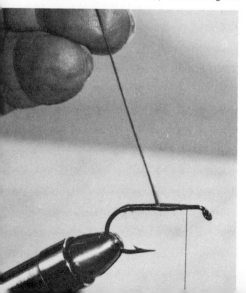

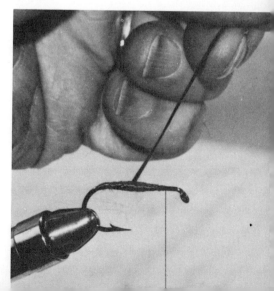

Herl Body

A herl body is formed by tying in as a clump several strands of herl selected for uniformity in length. Tie in the butts just below the point where the quills begin to become fully fuzzed (left). Anchor the butts with extra turns of the thread and clip them, then twist the herl into a single strand by rolling it in one direction between thumb and fingers (right). Wrap as you would floss or wool or any other standard material. Keep the twist in the herl as you wrap. Tie off at the desired point with two or three turns of thread and clip.

A herl body must be stranded as it is formed. To tie a herl body, select enough strands of approximately equal length and texture to form a body of the desired bulk. This number will vary with hook size and the quality of herl you're working with. On the #10 wide-gap hook in the picture, six strands are used, but a #14 hook would probably need only two or three strands, and a single strand of very thickly fuzzed herl might serve for a #16 or #18 hook. Hold the herl in a compact roll when you tie it in, and be sure to tie far enough down on the material so that the butts of the strands, which are usually less thickly covered than the center portions, are above the tie. Trim the protruding ends, then twist the herl strands together to make a single thick strand that is wound on the hook. You may have to give the herl another slight twist or two as you carry the body toward the hook eye, to keep them firmly together. Finish and tie off just as you would any other body material.

Forming a quill body is basically the same process, regardless of the kind of quill used. In the accompanying pictures, it's condor feather fiber quill, and the first step is to select and cut a strand that is long enough to form a body on the #12 hook it will be wound on. A bit of experience will make this easier. Tie in the quill as far toward its butt end as possible, grip the butt with hackle pliers and wrap on so that the turns touch. Tie off in the usual manner.

118

Quill Body

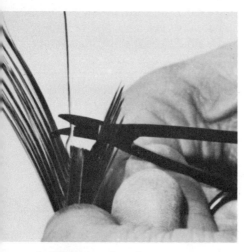

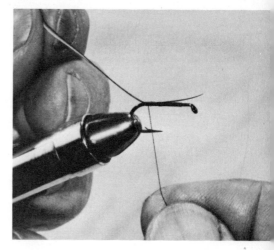

1. This is a section of condor wing, which has long, loosely interlocked fibers. Cut one fiber for a small hook, two for a large one. Large is #12 or better.

2. Tie in the quill by its tip; practice will teach you how much you must leave to fill the hook. Trim excess tip material.

3. Use hackle pliers to hold the quill butt while wrapping it in even turns along the hook shank. The turns should touch.

4. Tie off the quill and trim in the usual manner after anchoring it with one or two safety turns of the thread.

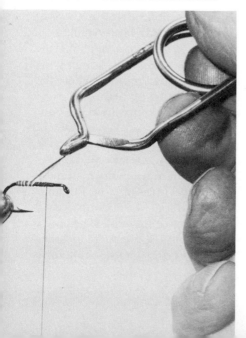

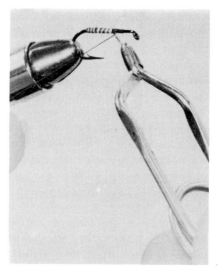

While there are several kinds of quill that give a two-tone effect, as does the condor feather fiber, and while it's possible to get a striped body by wrapping two quills of different colors on the hook, you'll sometimes want colored quill bodies. Dyeing white or cream-colored quills is one way of getting a colored body, but an easier way is to use white or light-hued quill and after wrapping the body use a felt-tipped pen to get the shade desired. These pens are available in virtually any color and shade you might need, and give the quills a translucent color that dye doesn't achieve. The ink in these pens is waterproof, in case you wondered.

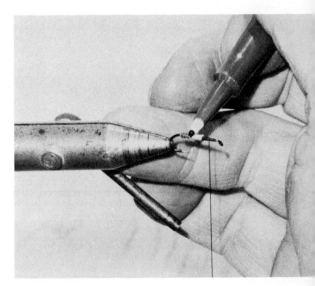

For a colored quill body, use a white or cream-colored quill and after wrapping, color the quill with a felt-tipped pen.

None of the variations of standard body construction call for methods of handling materials or procedures that have not already been detailed. In the forming of butted and jointed bodies ribbing is applied simply by tying in the ribbing material just before tying in the body material, bringing the ribbing up the body in a neat spiral and tying it off at the point where the body ends. A butt joint aft is tied in, wrapped and tied off before the body material is tied in; a butt joint fore is formed at the point where the body material is tied off.

A center joint is only slightly more complicated. The body is wrapped to the point where the center joint will begin, and the material is tied off but not clipped. Instead, the joint material is tied in, and the body material is pulled along the hook shank and held with several turns of tying thread at the spot where the body will be resumed. The material of the center joint is then wrapped, tied off and clipped, and the body is completed. If ribbing is being used it is handled just like the body material. If trailers are included in the pattern, the hackle wisps for them are tied in before the joint is wrapped.

Forming a dubbed body was covered in an earlier part of this chapter, and the variations required in forming tinsel and bucktail bodies will both be described in the chapter on streamer flies. Otherwise all the operations common to all flies have been detailed in this section, with one exception: finishing off the head. Throwing a couple of half hitches around the line-end of a fly isn't a very good way to end your tying job. Let's look now at easy ways to finish off your flies by taking what is the final step, tying a neat head. There are a couple of tools that will help you do this, or you can do the job by hand.

Probably the most commonly used whip-finishing tool is the Thompson. To use it, hold the tool with the tip of its spring-loaded arm upright, carry the thread from the hook to the tip of the fixed arm, around the spring-loaded arm and back across the top of the shaft. Rotate the entire tool clockwise one half-turn, put the humped tip of the shaft against the hook, bring the tying thread down parallel with and up against the hook and rotate the tool clockwise for four or five turns while maintaining tension on the thread. Disengage the fixed tip on the tool's shaft from hook and thread while still holding the thread under tension with the spring-loaded tip. Pull the thread to close the loop, holding the spring-loaded tip until this tip reaches the hook eye, then release the tip by slipping it out of the loop and pull the thread until the loop is closed. Clip the thread close.

You'll have to make the second type of whip-finishing tool yourself, but it takes only a couple of minutes. Using about 1 inch of size C or D tying thread, form a loop and whip it with 0 or 00 thread to the tip of a cocktail toothpick. Finish the whipping with a pull-through such as that used in winding rods. Varnish the whipped end, including the loop of heavy thread. You can make this kind of tool in several sizes, using different weights of thread for the loop, so as to have one for large flies and another for small ones.

To use the tool, lay the loop on the almost-completed fly head with the closed end toward the hook eye. Finish the head with four or five turns, cut the thread, leaving about 1 inch of extra length. Put the end of the tying thread through the tool's loop and pull the toothpick back toward the hook shank until the end of the tying thread is clear. Pull the tying thread tight and clip close.

Tying a whip-finish knot by hand is really easier than using a tool. When the fly head lacks only a few turns for completion, pick up the tying thread with two fingers of your right hand, holding the spool or bobbin in your left, and pull upward with your right hand to put the thread in a U-shaped line, the closed portion of the U being formed by your right-hand fingers. Bring your left hand up behind the length of thread between fingers and hook; the thread will at this point look like a reversed figure 4. Bring up the thumb of your right hand to grasp the loop as you let it slip off your fingers; hold what had been the vertical line of the reversed 4 between the thumb and forefinger of your right hand while dropping the thread with your left hand to hug the hook shank. Keeping the loop open, make four

Whip Finish with Thompson Tool

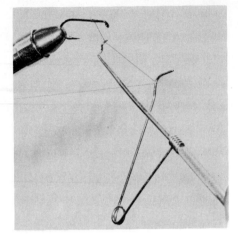

1. To use the Thompson whip-finish tool, pass the thread from the hook over both curved tips and pull the thread back toward the vise. Hold tool with the spring of its spring-loaded tip pointing down.

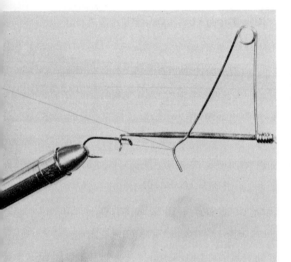

2. Rotate the shaft one half-turn clockwise. The spring now points up and the thread is behind the shaft. Put the fixed tip against the hook and turn the tool clockwise. Don't let the spring-loaded tip take on too much tension, especially if you're using fine thread, or the thread might break.

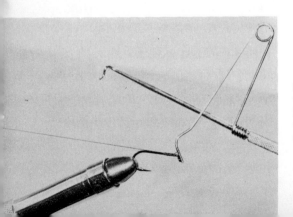

3. When the head is formed, slip the fixed tip off the hook and pull the thread at the bobbin to bring the spring-loaded tip to the hook eye, slip the tip out, pull the loop tight and trim.

Whip Finish with Homemade Tool

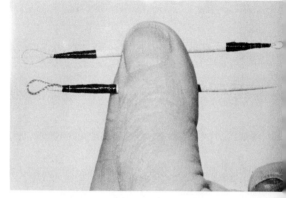

1. Construction of these homemade whip-finish tools is described in the text. You can use different-sized thread and make loops of several sizes to handle any size of flies.

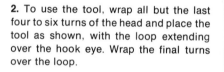
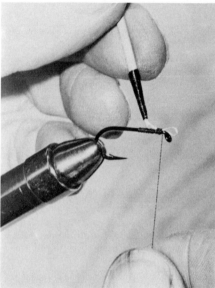

2. To use the tool, wrap all but the last four to six turns of the head and place the tool as shown, with the loop extending over the hook eye. Wrap the final turns over the loop.

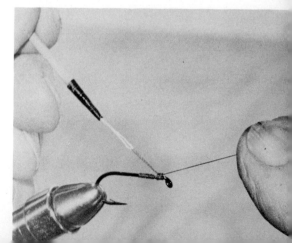

3. Cut the tying thread, leaving about 1 inch of excess length. Pass the end of the thread through the loop, tweak the tool backward toward the fly's body, pulling the tying thread under the wraps taken around the loop. Pull the tying thread tight before clipping it.

No-tool Whip Finish

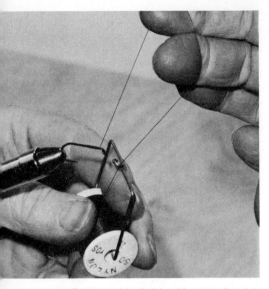

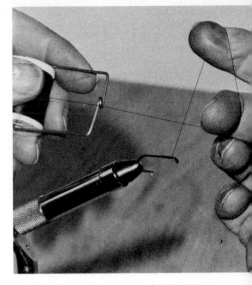

1. To tie a whip-finish without tools, pick up the tying thread with the forefinger of your right hand when only a few turns need be wrapped to finish off the head.

2. Bring the bobbin up so that the loop becomes a reversed figure 4, with the thread from the bobbin going *behind* the thread that forms the upright line of the reversed 4.

3. Grasp the vertical thread between the forefinger and thumb of your right hand, letting the loop slip off your fingers. Wrap formerly vertical thread around the hook, over the portion of thread leading to the bobbin.

4. Complete the wrapping without disturbing the loop, then slip the point of the bobbin into the loop and pull the thread in your left hand to close the loop. Trim off the thread, apply cement.

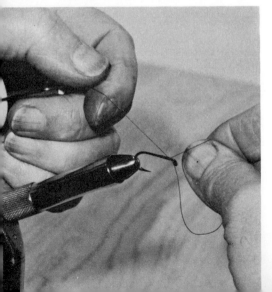

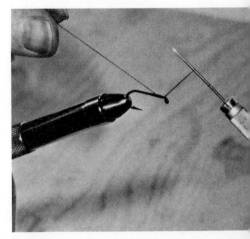

or five turns around the top of the hook, passing each turn over the thread held in your left hand. Release the loop, pick up your bodkin and slip its point into the loop. Maintain tension on the loop with the bodkin while pulling the loop closed with your left hand. When the loop slips off the point of the bodkin and closes completely, pull tight and clip off.

You will, of course, apply a coat or two of head lacquer to the heads to give your flies that "well-dressed" look.

Now let's move along from the general procedures common to tying all flies and examine those that are used in tying the wings and hackle that typify and distinguish the different kinds of flies.

10

Dry Flies

WHEN I FIRST BEGAN fly fishing, more years ago than I like to recall, divided quill wings were the standard dry-fly dressing. Once in a while some venturesome angler would bend on a fanwing or spentwing dry, but the hairwing dry fly was not often seen, and the rolled-wing fly was extremely rare. Beginning during the 1960s, the rolled wing rapidly gained popularity and is, I'm sure, the dominant type of dry-fly winging today. I still like drys with quill wings and still take fish on them consistently, even though a lot of other anglers look on them as quaint antiques. To have a balanced fly box, I think a fisherman needs a sample of any fly that might attract a fish, so I'll keep my divided quill wings, though now they're nudging five or six other styles of winging in my overcrowded box.

Actually, the divided quill, the hackle-tip wing, the fanwing, the rolled wing, and the hairwing dry flies should share almost equal honors as fish-takers. No box is complete without all of them. And there are a few other styles of dry that need to be included, for who knows what vagary might be lurking in the minds of the fish the next time you go out to wet a line?

WINGING TECHNIQUES

Let's start our winging of dry flies with an examination of the quills used in the operation. They will be from the primary wing feathers or the tail and will be sturdy without being thick, soft without being mushy, and the barbules between each fiber will be springy enough to mesh together and lock the fibers securely in place. To wing a fly properly you need matched right and left quills, and from each one you will cut a section containing from six to twelve fibers, depending on the size of the hook being used. These sections will, ideally, come from approximately the same area of both wings. Drawing the tip of your bodkin between the fibers will isolate the sections so that you can cut them out.

Winging a Fly

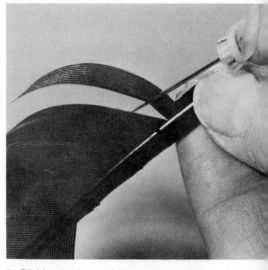

1. Matched quills for winging must be in pairs, right and left, the curves of both quill and feather fibers being opposite one another.

2. Divide sections of fibers from each wing by drawing the point of the bodkin between the fibers; cut the sections out close to the quill

3. Match the fiber sections by putting their tips together so that the outward flare of the tips will be on opposite sides of the fly. Measure against the hook for length to find the tie-in point.

4. Bring the thread over the near feather, down between it and the hook, under the hook and up between hook and the far feather, then over the tops of the feather pieces and below the hook.

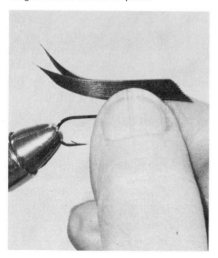

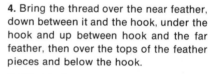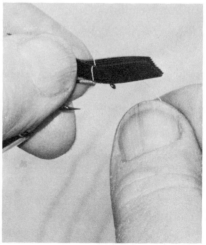

Continued

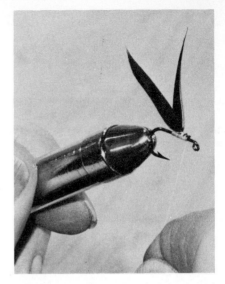

5. Make an extra turn or two with the thread to bind the feather sections to the hook. Bring the thread between the feathers and hook from behind and pull gently forward, then add a few turns of thread to make the shoulder.

6. Trim excess fibers ahead of the thread and wrap over the remaining stubs. Your finished wings should look like this. Remember, the scale is exaggerated somewhat for photographic clarity.

Purists and traditionalists maintain that the wings of a dry fly should stand as high as the hook shank is long. This is fine if your objective is just to tie pretty, symmetrical-looking flies, but it seems to me to ignore the purpose of the fly, which is to resemble an insect on which the fish you're after feed. Make the wings as long or as short as they need to be to give you the best imitation. If your fly imitates nothing, then make the wings in fine proportions if it suits your pleasure.

When your fly is ready to be winged, match the tips of your quill fibers from their natural points, with the curve of the feather inward, so that the tips flare out on each side of the fly's body. Place them from the eye, holding the strips over the hook until you can grasp the tips between your left thumb and forefinger. Bring the tying thread up on the outside of the near-side wing, down along the feather on its inner surface, under the hook, up over the far-side wing from its inner surface, down over the outer surface, and under the hook again. The two loops if viewed head-on would look like the letter M, with the near-side wing in the angle of the letter's left side, the far-side wing in the right-side angle, the hook shank just over the middle V. Pull the tying thread up from the hook shank, pulling almost straight up, to bind the wing fibers as the threads pull the sections down and compress them on the hook. Take an extra turn with the thread around the shank, using the bodkin to make any adjustments required in the set of the wings. Then loop the thread horizontally around the back of the wings, as close to their base as you can manage, and pull the wings upright to the angle you desire. You may have to take another loop or two in order to get the stand that pleases you most. Clip the excess from the front of the wings and make several wraps with the thread to reduce the bulk of the stubs of fiber left after trimming and to bind the wings firmly to the hook.

When you attach divided quill wings in this manner, you'll find the M-loop hard to manage at first, but it gets easier with very little practice. The horizontal loops behind the wings allow you to control the degree of set; you can bring the wings upright if you choose, cock them forward, or let them slant back over the body at any angle you wish. By adding a cross-bind between the wings you can also control the degree of flare.

Hackle tips make excellent dry-fly wings in spite of their apparent fragility; they're especially effective when tied spent. The first step in winging a dry fly in this fashion is to trim out matching tips from a pair of good neck hackles; you'll usually find a pair just a bit oversize for hackling which will make ideal wings. Trim the tips long enough to give you plenty of quill to work with.

When clipping hackle tips for spentwings, allow yourself plenty of quill at the butt ends. You can strip excess fibers and trim quill ends, but you can't stretch the quill if it has been cut too short.

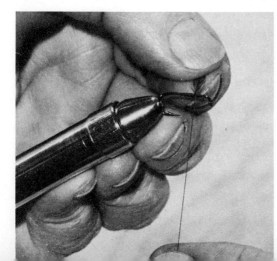

Set one wing at a time after matching the hackle tips. Hold the quill across the hook on top of the shank at right angles and use a loop to anchor it in place as you set the other wing.

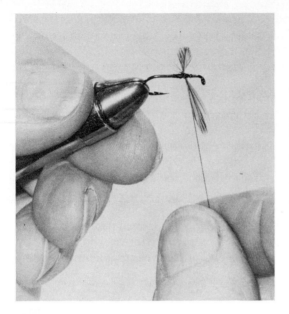

When setting the second wing, bring your loop down to cross over and behind the loop that set the first wing. Then, when making anchor wraps, adjust the set of the wings by criss-crossing the thread, squeezing the wings with it as needed. Anchor the wraps with a drop of head cement before finishing the fly.

After stripping the fibers to bring the hackle tips to the desired size, tie in one wing, using a cross-tie to set it in place. Then tie in the opposite wing in the same fashion. You can if necessary loop the tying thread horizontally around the wing base to lift the tips if they tend to droop more than they should.

Setting a pair of fanwings precisely isn't a matter of luck but depends on your ability to select the right pair of feathers from which to take the tips. Once you've matched the curve and fiber formation in the breast or side-feathers from almost any waterfowl, it's a relatively easy job to place the wings. Leave yourself plenty of quill when you begin removing strips of fiber to match the tips in size. A few fibers too many in one of the two wings will result in a lopsided, badly floating fly.

Holding the wings, matched at their tips, in your left hand, lower them over the hook shank to straddle it, one quill on either side, and loop the tying thread around both quills. At this stage, the feathers should be slanted very slightly back toward the bend of the hook. Tighten the thread firmly and make a second loop, passing the thread behind the quills and pulling it forward as you tighten it while bringing it under the hook shank. Using the tip of the bodkin or tweaking very, very gently with your finger-tips, adjust the set of the wings. To complete the tie, bring the thread be-tween the wings, forward, then in the reverse direction; the thread will describe an X or a figure 8, both of which names are applied to this tie. By using the pressure of the thread against the base of the wings you can ad-just their angle and set quite precisely with only three or four wraps of the thread.

Tying in Fanwings

1. Selecting well-matched feathers is the key to good fanwings. As when tying spentwings, leave plenty of butt quill to work with when cutting the wings from the tip of a body feather.

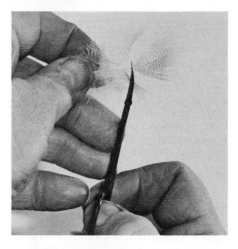

2. Pair the feathers between your left thumb and forefinger, and once you've got them mated, don't let go until they're tied in. Lower the quills over the hook, straddling the shank, and tie in with a double loop, passing the first turn from front to back, the next from back to front. Make a couple of similar turns to anchor the quills; you can do some minor adjusting of the set as you do this.

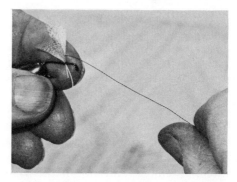

3. Final adjustment of the set is made by passing the thread between the feathers from back to front, then carrying the thread down under the hook, bringing it up in front of the wings and passing it between them from front to back. This is the figure-8 or X tie, and you can usually adjust wings with about two crisscrosses in each direction.

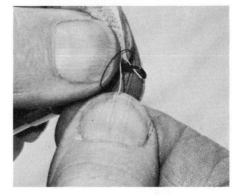

4. This is how your finished wings ought to look, flaring in symmetrical arcs above the hook.

Tying in Rolled Wings

1. Rolled wings are tied from a single body or breast feather; it should be oversized in relation to the hook used. Match up the sides by stripping bottom fibers from each side until the fibers are equal on both sides.

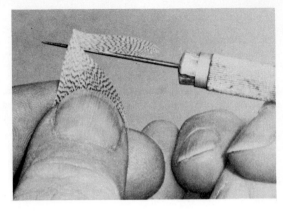

2. Clip out the tip of the feather just below the end of the quill. Your finished feather will look like this.

Tying rolled wings differs from tying fanwings in that selection of the feather used is less important than your ability to manipulate the tying thread. You should choose a large feather in relation to hook size, as roughly one-third of the feather will be trimmed away or wrapped under. After selecting the feather to be used, trim out its center, taking out a length of quill approximately a third as long as the amount of fibered quill remaining. Fold the feather into a V with the quill at its apex and roll it between forefinger and thumb into a compact cylinder. Place the cylinder on the hook shank with the quill next to the hook and make two turns around it with the thread at the point where the base of the wings will be in the finished fly.

Grasp the forward portion of the fibers ahead of the tying thread and pull them back along the shank, then form a shoulder on the shank ahead of the fibers. Make five or six wraps, enough to push the feather upright

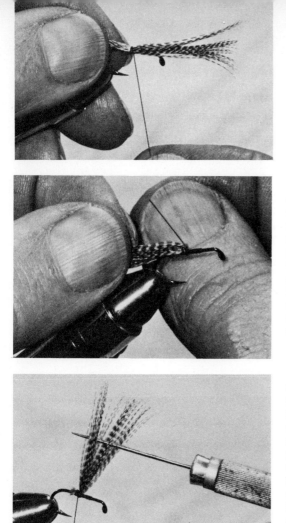

3. Roll the feather between your fingers into a compact cylinder. Place the cylinder on the hook shank as shown, with the fiber ends protruding beyond the eye. Tie in with a loop and two anchor turns.

4. Pinch the fibers together with thumb and forefinger ahead of the tie-in point and pull them back, folding over the thread. Hold them parallel to the shank while forming a shoulder against them by making several turns of the thread, building it up from the hook to press against the feather and hold the fibers upright.

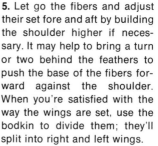

5. Let go the fibers and adjust their set fore and aft by building the shoulder higher if necessary. It may help to bring a turn or two behind the feathers to push the base of the fibers forward against the shoulder. When you're satisfied with the way the wings are set, use the bodkin to divide them; they'll split into right and left wings.

and hold it there. Release the fibers, add more thread to the shoulder if necessary, and while doing this, make two or three wraps behind the fibers to push them forward against the shoulder formed in front of them. Then, divide the fibers along their natural division line with the point of your bodkin; they will help by springing into place as you comb the bodkin through them. Next, use the X or figure-8 tie, carrying the thread through the divided wings and around their base, pulling in stray wisps of fiber as you work, to bring the wings together and give them the proper set. Tie off and apply a drop of cement on the wrappings to prevent the fibers from straying later on.

We'll look in the next chapter at other styles of winging that are more closely associated with wet flies than dry. There will be some further details in this chapter about winged dry flies in special patterns, but first let's look at hackling a dry fly.

HACKLING TECHNIQUES

That you need good hackle, sparsely fibered feathers from the neck of a well-aged rooster or gamecock, was established in an earlier chapter, as was the need for hackle to match hook size. The formula followed by most tiers is that dry-fly hackle should be no more than one and a half times as long as the hook shank. Remember, we're talking now about standard dry-fly hackle; there are variations from standard, which we'll cover later. Moreover don't take any formula dealing with fly tying too literally, allow yourself some leeway. The dry-fly hackle "formula" isn't gospel or a Supreme Court decision. It doesn't mean that every fiber of a dry fly's hackle feather must be of equal length, so if a few fibers are a bit longer, don't stay awake at night worrying about it.

Generally, dry-fly hackle should be quite dense so that the fly will float well. To achieve this, it's common practice to use two hackles on a dry fly. After stripping away the webbed portion of the hackle feathers and stroking the fibers backwards as described in the preceding chapter, tie in one hackle behind the wings, the other ahead of them. Tie in the front hackle with its shiny side toward the hook eye, the rear hackle with its shiny side toward the rear.

Wrap the front hackle first, taking the first turn or two in back of the wings; then angle the hackle to pass in front of the wings for the remaining turns. Tie off the feather and clip away the excess. Next, wrap the second hackle, again taking the first turns behind the wings, and as you angle this hackle forward toward the hook eye, fill any voids or bare spots left when the first one was wrapped. Tie off and clip the second hackle, taking an extra security turn or so with the thread when tying off. Use the bodkin to pick out wrapped-under fibers and put on a drop of cement as an extra precaution.

While dry-fly fishermen differ on many aspects of the sport, there's one thing on which all of them agree: a dry fly is useless unless it floats well. This consideration takes me back to an incident that occurred many years ago, while I was fishing a long fast-water stretch on the Gallatin. The water was high and its riffled surface turbulent, and I was having trouble keeping my flies afloat. Silicone and other modern floatants lay far in the future; the best then available was mucilin, which all my fishing mentors had advised me not to use unless it was necessary. This day, it was necessary, but I'd left the bottle behind and was fishing alone, and I'd seen nobody on the river who might lend me a dab or two.

Finally giving up, I walked along the bank looking for calmer water, but before reaching any saw another fly fisherman working the same kind of rough surface that had defeated me. When I got close enough to watch his casts, I could see his fly bobbing saucily erect on the currents that had swallowed mine as soon as they touched down. While I watched, he took a nice fish and waded to shore. We began talking, and as soon as was decently possible I worked the conversation around to the long floats he was getting and asked what kind of floatant he was using.

Hackling a Dry Fly

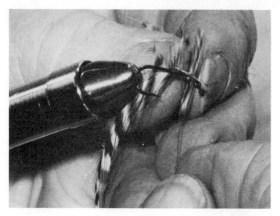

1. Dry-fly double hackles are tied in separately, the front with its shiny or outer face toward the hook eye, the other with its inner or dull side facing forward.

2. Wrap the front hackle first, taking turns in front of and behind the wings. When the first hackle has been tied in and its end clipped, wrap the rear feather.

3. After wrapping a turn or so of the second hackle back of the wings, wrap it forward, filling in voids or thin spots left after the first hackle was wrapped. After tying off this hackle, use the bodkin to pick out fibers that have been caught under the quills of the two hackles.

135

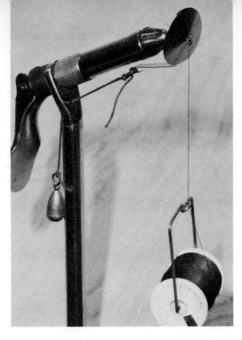

A hackle guard helps to keep fibers out of the way when finishing the fly's head.

He countered with a question, asking if I tied my own flies. I admitted that I'd recently started tying, and he said: "I'll tell you, then. Tie in a couple of antelope or elk hairs in the tails and three or four in the hackle, and your dry flies will float without any oiling." To prove his point, the stranger—whose name I forgot long ago—gave me a couple of local patterns from his box, which I used without a sink until I lost them later in the day in the jaws of a pair of trout that I couldn't handle.

Since then, I've added a few of these hollow-cored hairs to any dry fly that I might possibly use on a fast-water stream, using antelope in patterns calling for light hackle, elk in those with dark. I've never had a fish object to me breaking a pattern by including such extraneous material in the dressing, nor have I been bothered by having flies sink in fast water.

There's no trick involved in putting in the hairs. Adding a couple or three to the tail is easy, and it's almost equally easy to stick in five or six at the time you set the butts of the hackle in place. Of course, when wrapping the hackle you want to be careful not to wrap the hairs under. This, incidentally, is one way to get a high-floating dry fly with very sparse hackle.

You're now ready to form the fly's head, and you want to avoid catching the thread on stray hackle fibers. Some tiers simply pull back the front layers of fibers with their fingertips and hold them until the head is ready to be whip-finished. Others like to use a hackle guard, a metal shield with a split to allow it to be attached and removed without disturbing the tying thread. It is for the tier to determine which he prefers to use, his fingers or the guard.

Now, about those variations from "standard" dry-fly hackling. There are only three that are important. The first is dressing a fly with Palmered hackle. This simply involves tying in the tip of a hackle at the butt and winding it up the body in much the same way as you add ribbing. It must be

136

understood that Palmered hackle isn't a fly pattern, but a style of tying hackling. Any fly pattern can be dressed with Palmered hackle. However, any Palmered fly with the hackle simply wrapped along the body over the tying thread is called a "Brown Palmer" or "Grey Palmer" or whatever the hackle might be.

Next, we come to bivisibles. This again is a style of hackling and not a pattern, even though there is a family like that of Palmered flies that are all-hackle flies tied bivisible, which simply means that a strip of contrasting colored hackle has been added to the face of the regular hackle. You can dress any fly you choose to as a bivisible by doing this.

Finally, there's variant hackling, which is using hackle that is about 50 percent longer than the "standard" of one and a half times the length of the hook shank. Again, any pattern can be tied with variant hackling. Many fly fishermen and tiers think of variant hackling as being new, but it's been around for a century or so, having been originated in 1875 by Dr. William Baigent, a noted British dry-fly innovator. Variant hackling should not be confused with variant hackle, which is a term applied to off-color or other than standard-color hackle feathers.

An example of variant hackling in flies is the Spider family, which are flies dressed on very short hooks with very long, very sparse hackle. The accompanying pictures illustrate the Spider dressing, and the pattern listings in the last chapter give pattern details.

A spider is an example of variant hackling as well as of the flies belonging to this family. The body is a wrap or two of floss on the Mustad spider hook.

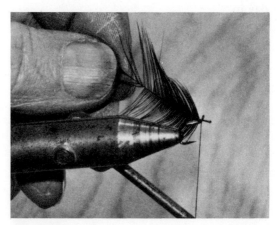

Spider hackling is sparse—two turns, three at most—and, like variant hackle, overlong in relation to the gap of the hook.

There are two special flies in the dry family that must be noted before this chapter ends. One is the detached body fly designed to imitate the mayflies that are so fascinating to Eastern fly fishermen. The naturals of the mayfly group have fairly full, upswept wings and bodies with high, pointed abdomens that curve upward from the thorax. Fly tiers have spent countless hours trying to come up with a successful imitation of these flies and are only now beginning to succeed. For a long while the best imitation mayfly bodies were those made of a self-adhering plastic material, thin and translucent, that was cut so that when pinched together over a hook it resembled the natural insect's body.

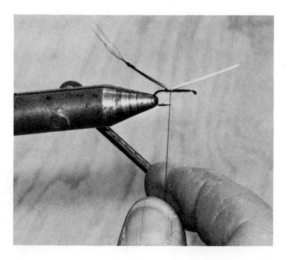

A length of porcupine quill, hollowed of its pith, with three moose-mane tips whipped to its pointed end (the point and barb of the quill are cut off, by the way) is tied and shouldered behind to create the mayfly detached body type of fly.

Wings on mayfly imitations are fibers from the thin bottom portion of a mallard quill, tied divided and low, straddling the hook. Place the fiber sections with the shank between them and tie in with a simple loop.

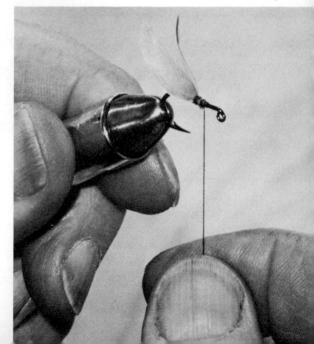

Vincent Marinaro in his *A Modern Dry Fly Code* gives the dressing that is the best solution so far: an imitation of the insect's upcurving body using a length of porcupine quill hollowed out with the fine blade of a jeweler's saw and having three moose-mane hairs whipped to the tip of the quill. The accompanying picture shows the body as created by Marinaro, in my interpretation. Marinaro suggests wings of blue-dun hackle tied half-spent; I'd be the last to argue with this scholarly and creative angler, but I like better a wing of the very thinnest bottom fibers of a mallard flight quill tied astride the hook shank, as shown in the second series of photos.

One final note before we leave dry flies. We may see the time when hackling a dry fly is something that was done "in the good old days" before polypropylene wool entered the angling picture. This wool has a specific gravity less than that of water, so it will float unsupported by the tips of hackle feathers. As this is written, the material — usually abbreviated to "poly-yarn" — is still too new to be evaluated in terms of its ultimate impact on flies. Tiers and anglers all over the land are experimenting with it, evolving changes in old patterns and inventing new ones that will allow this poly-wool to earn its place or be relegated to obscurity.

It's a fascinating material, though, and quite an experience to see a hackle-free fly floating merrily in a swift riffle. My own tests of poly-wool are negligible, but my few trials in the lakes and small streams of California's Sierra Nevadas during 1974 indicate that it's well worth working with. If you want to experiment, poly-wool is available in both yarn and unstranded fibers for dubbing. Just tie your flies made from it with no hackles — unless you want to follow the example of the fellow who wore both a belt and suspenders, and add the hackle "just in case."

11

Wet Flies

THESE ARE THE ancestors with which fly fishing began, so we must remember to treat them with due respect. As one of my fishing companions used to say acidly: "The dry fly gets the glamor, but the wet fly gets the fish." From a purely statistical standpoint, he's probably right, for the wet-fly family is far more numerous than the dry, if you include its popular branches, the streamer and nymph. We will include these, of course, but in another chapter. At the moment, we're interested only in the versions of the wet fly that for lack of a better term must be described as "conventional" or "standard."

Most fly fishermen and tiers are more meticulous about the patterns and form of their wet flies than they are about those of drys. Their belief is that a fish has more time to study the wet fly than it does the floating dry, and that consequently color and form are much more important in wets. The theory may well be right, but as was pointed out earlier, we still don't know precisely how a fish sees things, how acute its color perception is, and we're not always sure exactly how the materials we put on a hook dry look when they're underwater.

This was brought home to me many years ago, when it was my habit to spend a month each spring fishing a lake in the northern Sierras. The fish were mostly browns, and while the dry fly drew its share of action, the ace-in-the-hole fly for fishermen who knew the water well was a leadwing version of the Bluebottle, tied with a deep blue chenille body. The lake was singularly free from snags and until mid-July had no underwater vegetation into which a hooked fish could dive and break off, and given reasonable skill in handling a rod, the angler was generally able to bring most of his hooked fish to the net.

One year during my June sojourn there, I hit a fantastic spell of action. It began on a day when I hooked, netted, and released over twenty fish, and I continued during the next few days at much the same pace. Oddly, I didn't lose a fly during those first five or six days, nor did I change from the one I had on when the streak started. After about a week, though, the original fly began to look chewed and battered, so I bent on another of the same pattern. And the action came to a grinding halt. An occasional nudge, a strike or two, but nothing to compare with what it had been. Switching flies didn't help until I went back to the battered specimen with which I'd started.

As you may have anticipated, strikes began coming fast again and continued as long as I used the bedraggled fly, which by this time was beginning to come apart. This didn't seem to bother the fish. For about three weeks the fishing was fantastic, then it stopped as abruptly as it had begun. To this day, I don't know how much credit the fly gets; all I can be sure of is that as long as it was on my leader I got tremendous action. But I have a theory that there was something about the coloring of the fly, either the body material, wings, hackle, or ribbing, that was fatally fascinating to those brown trout — even though it may have been a phenomenon confined to that one lake at that specific time. It never happened again, in case you're curious.

WINGING TECHNIQUES

Fish stories are fine, and it's nice to recall good fishing days, but we've strayed from our objective, which is tying wet flies. The winged wet fly of the past was typically dressed with downwings, though today the style of dressing favors hairwings tied at a somewhat higher angle to the body. Since the preliminary steps are the same as those already detailed for the divided quill wing, we can go at once to getting them on the hook.

After trimming your matched sections of fibers from a pair of quills of the appropriate size and color, match the sections at the tips, with the curvature to the outside. Holding the wings above the hook shank, bring the tying thread up over the wings, down and back toward yourself between the bottom of the wings and the hook, then over the wings and back under the hook. Tighten the thread very slowly and hold the wings firmly while guiding them down on the hook as the looped thread compresses the fibers and pulls the wing sections down into place at the same time. This ensures that when the thread is fully tight the wings will sit squarely atop the hook shank. After making a couple of safety turns and trimming the butts of the fibers, you're ready for hackle.

Flatwinged wet flies are seldom seen today, but this style of winging most closely resembles the wing attitude of a drowned insect floating underwater. To tie flatwings, choose the customary pair of fiber sections, preferably from quills in which the fibers do not curve sharply, such as a wide turkey or goose quill. Match the sections at their tips with the fiber sections atop one another, the top edges on opposite sides, and carefully spread them apart at the tips so that the top edge of the upper section will be on the right-hand side of the fly. Use your thumb and forefinger as a swivel while making this separation; you will wind up with the sections flat in a V shape, with the butt ends at the apex.

Tying Downwings

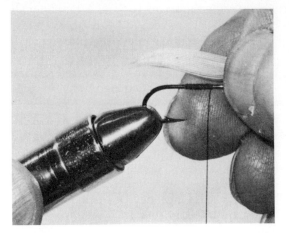

1. Match paired feather fiber sections for downwing flies at the tips, the curves of the fibers' center portion on the outside.

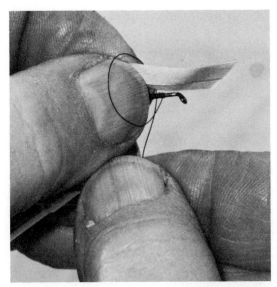

2. Tie the wings in with a double loop: bring the thread up and over the wings, between wings and hooks, and over the wings again, behind and under the hook. Form the loops loosely and pull closed while holding the wings so that they will be pulled down on top of the hook.

3. Properly tied, no shouldering should be needed behind the wings to make them set above the body. If shouldering is needed, it should not raise the wings too high.

Tying Flatwings

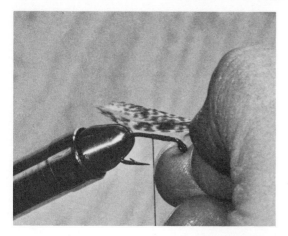

1. To start the tie-in for flatwing flies you'll have to use your left hand to handle the thread, for these wings go on most easily when positioned from the front, the right thumb and forefinger holding them as shown.

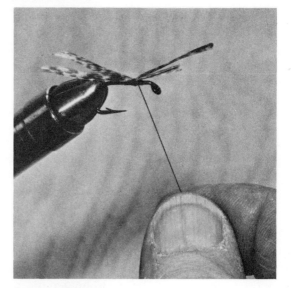

2. Use the double loop detailed in the preceding sequence of photos to tie in flatwings; these are set to lie close to the body.

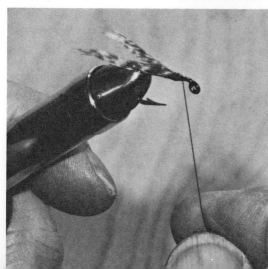

3. This is the way your finished flatwings should look.

Position the wings over the hook so that the point of the V is a bit further back on the shank than you would normally place wings being tied in. Bring the tying thread around the wings in the loop used to set downwings, and tighten. If alteration in the set of the wings is needed, it can be carried out with the bodkin while releasing the thread tension very slightly. Once the wings are set to your satisfaction, trim and tie off. You might try dressing this fly with the wings set about a third fore in a waisted body with the wings at the narrowed waist. Form the aft body first, set the wings, complete the body, and hackle very sparsely with the hackle tied in a semi-Palmer over the forebody.

Wet flies can be dressed with any style of wings you choose, including those detailed in earlier or later chapters for other kinds of flies. This being the case, we'd better move on to aspects of dressing wet flies that aren't discussed elsewhere.

HACKLING TECHNIQUES

Chief of these aspects is hackling. There are two approaches, full and throat, and unless a pattern specifies one or the other, the style in which a wet fly is hackled is the tier's choice. Wet-fly hackle is always softer and floppier than that put on dry flies, and is usually longer and tied to trail back over the hook.

Full hackle for a wet fly is tied in in the usual fashion, the quill butt clipped, and the quill secured with a couple of safety turns of the tying thread. The wrapping should be confined to three or four turns, or the fly's entire body will be concealed as it drapes back underwater. After the hackle has been tied off and the tip of the feather clipped, several turns of the tying thread should be made over the front fibers while they are pulled back along the fly's body. This will give them the backsweep characteristic of wet-fly hackles.

To form throat hackle, pull a bunch of fibers from a saddle hackle and without letting go of them roll the fibers into a compact cylinder between thumb and forefinger. Measure by holding the wisp of fibers under the fly at the angle they will assume when tied in; throat hackle on a wet fly traditionally extends beyond the point of the hook to the end of the bend and is tied at an angle to cover the point. Bring the hackle up under the hook with the tying thread behind the wisp, pull the thread over the hook and around the hackle, and take an extra turn for safety. To adjust the angle of the hackle in relation to the hook shank, use the thread as needed to form a shoulder behind the wisp, then clip excess fibers, tie off, and finish the head.

Hairwings are always good on wet flies, and the method of forming them is detailed in the following chapter, as is that for winging wet flies with hackle-feather and marabou streamer wings. You'll also find ways of weighting hooks in this chapter. And, for some reason that seems logical but inexplicable, the tying of nymphs is in the next chapter as well.

Full Hackling a Wet Fly

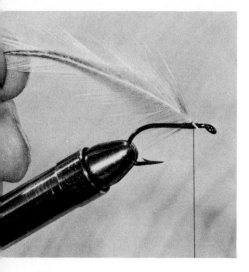 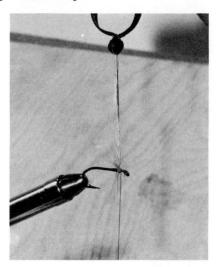

Full hackle for a wet fly is wrapped in much the same fashion as that for a dry fly, but is sparser, usually does not have any wraps back of the wings and is slightly backswept. Start by tying in the butt of the saddle hackle **(1)**. Since saddle-hackle fibers are heavier and thicker than those of neck hackle, make only two or three wraps and tie off **(2)**. After making the usual safety turns with the thread, smooth the hackle fibers back along the hook shank **(3)** and begin the fly's head by taking several turns over the fibers. This gives the characteristic backsweep of the wet-fly hackle (**4**).

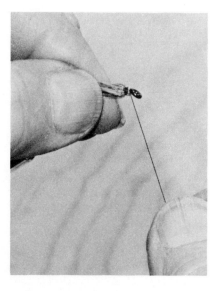 

Throat Hackling a Wet Fly

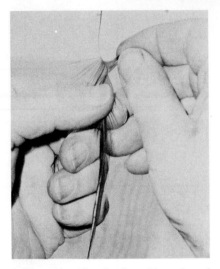

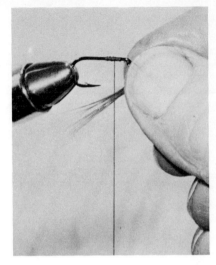

1. Throat hackling begins with a wisp of fibers pulled from the bottom of a saddle hackle. Roll the fibers into a cylinder without letting go of them.

2. Measure for length by holding the wisp of fibers under the hook; they should be long enough to cover point and barb.

3. Using your right hand to control the thread, bring the wisp up to the hook from below and tie in the hackle with a simple loop.

4. Adjust the set to the desired angle after taking the usual safety wrappings and clipping the fiber butts, forming a shoulder with the thread as needed just back of the hackle.

12

Streamer Flies and Nymphs

THERE'S NO REAL resemblance between the two types of flies this chapter brings together—big, elongated streamers and tiny nymphs—except that both are fished below the surface, which puts them together in the wet-fly family. Since the marriage has been made, though, let's allow it to stand and hope it'll be a happy one.

STREAMERS

Streamers fall into two chief categories, those with feather winging and those winged with hair. Technically, any hair-winged fly is a bucktail, even though the hair may never have been closer to a deer than the stockyard slaughterhouse. Both types go far back into history, for before anglers learned to wrap the head of a hook with hackle wound at right angles to the shank, they were tying the butts of feathers in at the heads of hooks and letting the quills stream out in minnowlike fashion. The bucktail is another of America's contributions to angling. In Canada, the Ojibways and Ottawas and in the southeastern part of the continent, the Tuscaroras and Catawbas are both recorded as fishing with strips of hair-out deer hide wrapped around hooks, and these records go back to the early 1800s.

Streamers are perhaps the easiest of all flies to tie. Most of them go on long, heavy hooks, 2x, 3x, and on up to 6x, which gives the tier a lot of room in which to manipulate materials and fingers. You have a lot of leeway in streamer patterns, too. Except in the case of salmon wet flies, which are technically streamers and which dedicated salmon fly fishermen inspect meticulously to be sure each fly contains all the features tradition demands, the tier can ad-lib pretty freely.

Streamer bodies trend to the more absorbent materials such as chenille and wool, and a lot of streamers have tinsel bodies that are easy and fast to form. When tying most streamers, especially those on the longer hooks, you'll find that using a heavier thread, certainly no lighter than 00, and even as heavy as A on big hooks, will speed your tying immensely, since it covers the big hooks with fewer turns. Aside from the difference in their size, there's no difference between streamers and other flies in such areas as forming bodies. You'll be using more material per body and may now and again underestimate the length of the floss or wool that you cut from the skein, and when you're forming herl bodies you'll probably have to tie in a second bunch of fibers about midway on a long hook. The bodies of all flies are formed pretty much the same way, though, given the difference between materials.

Winging with quill fibers is also quite similar, though you'll find yourself reaching more often for goose and turkey quills to get the length the long streamer hooks call for. Most streamers having quill wings are dressed in the downwing pattern detailed in the wet-fly chapter, so you can refer to it for tying-in data. In fact, the data provided in earlier chapters for any style of winging apply equally to streamer dressing.

A lot of streamer patterns call for saddle hackle wings, and these are among the easiest of all styles of wings to set. Match a pair of saddles of the proper size, putting their dull sides together and leaving yourself plenty of quill to work with. Position the feathers over the hook, push the quills down on the shank, and fix the feathers in place with simple turns of the tying thread. After the quills are firmly set on the shank, you can bring the thread behind and between quills and hook to form a one-thread-thick shoulder that will lift the hackles enough to ride above the body.

Marabou is another popular winging material for streamer flies, and setting wings of marabou is equally straightforward. There's a strong similarity between tying in marabou wing fibers and tying in floss that will help you do the job more easily. First, of course, you'll want to cut the wings, and for flies tied on extralong hooks this means clipping the fibers from the center of the quill, where they're the longest. Without letting go of the fibers, moisten the fingertips of your free hand and roll the butts together into a point, then tie in at the spot where the moistened portion ends. Use a simple over-the-hook loop to tie in with, take the usual two or three safety turns, clip the butts, and if you feel called on to do so, bring the thread between hook and feathers to clinch the tie more firmly.

When streamers call for peacock herl or sword wings or topping, use the marabou technique to make the tying-in easier. The method doesn't work well for quill strips, though; these feathers are generally from waterfowl, and even when they're from other birds they are moisture-resistant and tend to break down when you roll them.

Now, let's look at bucktails. Hair from the antlered species—deer, elk, antelope, caribou, and moose—is soft and relatively brittle. If you're putting any quantity on a hook, don't try to tie it all in at once, because if you put too much pressure on these hairs the tying thread might cut through the upper layers. Instead, add the hair a bit at a time. On the other hand, hair from bear, sheep, goats, calf—often called "kip" or "impala"—and most small animals such as foxes and squirrels is firm and resilient and can

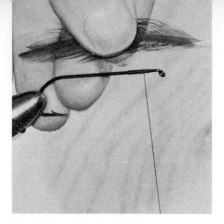

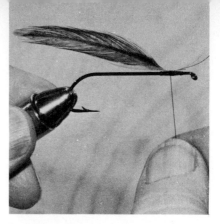

In setting saddle hackles for streamer-fly wings, match them at the tips, measure on the hook. The hackles should have their shiny, or good, sides out. Tie in with a simple loop.

A small shoulder, two or three turns of thread, usually lifts the hackles to ride above the fly body. Clip and tie off as usual.

be pulled down on pretty strongly without danger of cutting. Artificial polar bear hair, made from nylon or its cousin dynel, is also tough and very slippery. In fact, when tying in any hair it's wise to put a drop of head cement on the thread over the hair just as soon as it's firmly anchored to the hook. Remember, we're talking now about the long outer guard hairs of these animals, not the soft fur next to their skins that is used for dubbing; this is called underbody fur.

In fact, the underbody fur must be removed from the hair used as buck-tail wings, and the easiest way to do this is to clip a pinch of hair, going as close to the skin as you can and cutting off just enough to hold firmly between thumb and forefinger. Keep a firm grip on the pinch of hair and use the tip of the bodkin to comb out the underbody fur. Blowing through the cut ends of the hair while using the bodkin as a comb speeds up the clearing process.

A final step in preparing hair is jogging it to dislodge any final short shreds of underbody fur and to line up the cut ends evenly. There are a lot of ways to do this, one of them being by hand, but most tiers use some sort of cylindrical container just large enough to hold a pinch or two of hair. Lipstick cases are very popular, but I like the container I made from a short length of ½-inch diameter thin-walled plastic tubing. You can duplicate it in five minutes. Cut a 2-inch length of tubing, slice one end off at a slant, and shoulder a cork to fit into the straight end.

To use the jogger—this kind or any other—drop a pinch of cleaned hair in it, give it two or three sharp taps with your fingernail or tap the bottom on your bench several times, then lift out the hair from the top. If you're curious as to why I made one with a cork, I got tired of getting my eyes full of short bits of hair when I blew into the top of a lipstick case to clear loose underbody fur from the bottom. The cork allows the plastic tubing model to be wiped out.

Tying a Bucktail

1. Before starting to tie a bucktail, clear short, fuzzy underbody fur from the long guard hairs that will become the wings. Do this by holding firmly to the clipped tuft of hair and combing out the underbody fur with your bodkin.

2. Another important preliminary is "jogging" the cleaned hair to butt together the ends you'll tie in. A short piece of transparent plastic tubing with a cork cut to plug one end lets you see what you're doing and is easy to clean. To use it, drop the tuft of hair in and tap the cork several times on a firm surface.

3. When tying bucktails in layered colors, set each layer with the doubled loop detailed earlier, to keep the wings on top of the hook.

4. After tying in, set the hairwings as high as you wish by shouldering behind it.

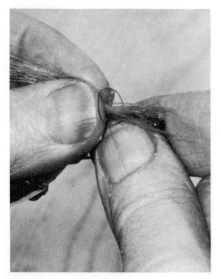

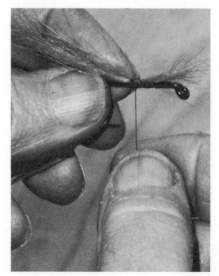

5. Always take the precaution of cementing hairwings and use enough cement to allow some to seep through the thread and fix the hairs.

6. Tie in succeeding layers as you did the first, positioning each layer just ahead of the previous one so that the earlier layers serve as shoulders.

When your pinch of hair is cleaned and its ends evened up, you're ready to attach it to the hook. Use the loop tie detailed in the chapter on wet flies, where its use is shown in the setting of downwings. It is a loop over the material, the thread being brought back between material and hook, then carried over the hook and tightened by pulling gently. The loop allows you to position your hairwings squarely on top of the hook shank, guiding it with your forefinger behind the hook as the thread is drawn up to close the loop and pull the hair down to the hook. Don't overlook the drop of cement after you've tied off the hair. We'll assume you're tying a wing with three different layers of colored bucktail, so while the cement dries, prepare the hair for the next layer.

Tie the second layer in just the tiniest fraction of an inch ahead of the first. This allows the lower layer to serve as a shoulder, forcing the one above it to stay in place. Repeat the operation with the third layer. Then you're ready to hackle the fly and give it a head.

While most streamers are tied on extralong, stout hooks, a lot of them — especially those with hairwings — need to be weighted so they will find bottom quickly and stay down in heavy currents. There are many materials that can be used for weighting. Thin shim metal, available from auto supply stores in 8 x 10-inch sheets, in brass, copper, and a pewter alloy, can be cut into thin strips and tied in like tinsel as an underbody. Shim metal is very flexible and easy to manipulate, as well as being readily available and quite inexpensive when you figure its cost per fly. It is also paper-thin, which is an advantage in forming thin fly bodies.

Lead wire is the most commonly used weighting material, but the lead wire usually available is quite large in diameter and makes for an unwieldy body. The most satisfactory material I've found is the very thin flexible lead used as a core in weighted trolling lines. It is of very small diameter, unusually malleable, and widely available. The core material from a 20-pound test trolling line makes an ideal hook weight. It's tied in and wrapped like any stranded body material and holds in place very well. When using lead wire of any kind, though, it's well to overwrap it with tying thread to make wrapping the body less of a chore. If you're working with a small-diameter thread, cut it after tying off the wire and knot on a heavier thread, such as size D or E, with which to make the overwrap, then go back to your regular thread to finish the fly.

Using the foregoing data and combining them with those in earlier chapters, and with the additional help of the pattern listing in the final chapter, you should have no trouble coping with any kind of streamer that you might want to tie.

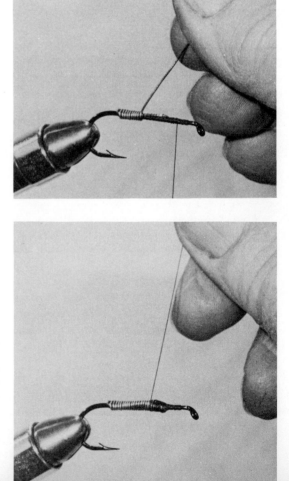

Lead wire or other metal used to weight a wet fly is tied in before any dressing materials. Wrap the hook with thread as usual, tie in the metal—in this case, lead wire from the core of an old piece of weighted line—and backwrap the thread to the front of the hook, stopping at the spot where the metal will be tied off. Wrap lead wire or other weighting metal closely along the shank.

After tying off and trimming the wire, backwrap the entire length of the shank, using the thread to fill spaces between turns of the wire and lay a smooth foundation for the body.

NYMPHS

Nymphs are perhaps the tier's greatest challenge. They must imitate the grubs and larvae they simulate much more closely than surface flies, or even wet flies, reproduce their models. Most nymphs are tiny, which means dressing them on very small hooks, and many of them call for numerous pieces of material as well as bodies that are flattened or otherwise altered from the round body typical of other flies.

Nymph specialists take great pains and pleasure in their precise imitations of naturals, and many of the nymphs created on tiny #20 to #28 hooks are true works of art that deserve the status of museum pieces. However, such detailed work isn't always necessary. Ray Bergman pointed this out in one of his books and listed a few very simple patterns that were consistent producers for him. When I tried some of these patterns I found that they worked as well in Western waters as they did in the Eastern streams and lakes for which Bergman created them.

One of the most consistently successful nymphs I've ever fished was of an almost laughably simple pattern; it was one that I created for the big Pacific Northwest steelhead rivers. These streams are not typical nymph water; they're silted regularly, which discourages larval life, and another discouraging factor is the constantly low water temperature. Most of the rivers do support a type of caddis that attaches its cases to the big rocks that line the riverbeds. My imitation of these cased larvae was a full, rounded body of light brown chenille with dark brown, sparse Palmered hackle, tied on #6, #8, and #10 heavy wire hooks. The nymph was one of my steelhead standbys for years and produced regularly for me and those of my companions who could bring themselves to try it. Most of my fishing friends, conditioned to big flashy flies on #2 and #4 hooks, shook their heads dubiously at the small, sloppy-looking nymph and stayed with their big flies even when they saw the nymph taking fish regularly. Old habits die hard.

Another very simple nymph pattern is one that I'd classify as being the most successful I've ever used for trout. On a #12 or #14 round-bend hook such as the Mustad 7948A, form a cylindrical body of dark orange or light red wool with fine gold ribbing. Before tying in the body and ribbing material, tie in a thin strip of grey quill fiber, and when the body is completed, bring this strip up over the back of the fly to lie flat and tie it off. With the bodkin point, fuzz out the butt fibers of the quill to imitate feelers, and as a final step give the quill fibers a coat or two of head cement.

Forming shaped nymph bodies — or bodies for large flies — has been greatly simplified by the appearance of a soluble floss. This looks and is handled like any other floss, but after it has been tied off a solvent applied with a fine brush will soften it and allow you to shape the body with a bodkin or flatten it with fine, thin-nosed pliers or tweezers. Flattened, waisted bodies can quickly and easily be formed in this fashion; so can detached bodies, since a strand of the floss dipped in the solvent and applied to the solvent-wettened body will adhere and while still wet can be formed into a mayfly body.

Tying a Hardback Nymph

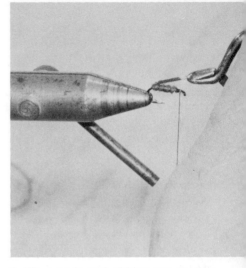

1. To tie what might be described as a prototype hardback nymph, common to most waters: in sequence, tie in a narrow strip of light grey quill fibers about four strands of fiber wide, narrow gold ribbing, and orange or light red crewel wool. Form the body of the wool.

2. When body and ribbing are on the hook, grasp the tip of the quill fiber with hackle pliers and bring it forward over the top of the body. Tie in but do not clip excess fibers.

3. Fuzz up the protruding quill butts with the bodkin and spread them on both sides of the body, set with a few turns of thread, clip the fibers to about $\frac{1}{16}$ to $\frac{1}{8}$ inch long to represent feelers.

4. Finally, give the fiber strip and head, including the feelers, a coat of cement.

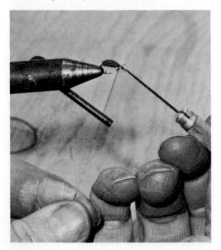

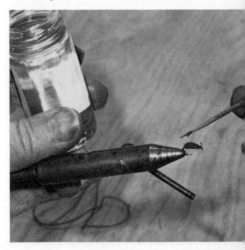

Many tiers, especially those new to the craft, are hesitant about trying their hand at nymphs because of the small hook sizes and the fineness of the materials used. In reality, a few hours spent in tying nymphs on hooks from #18 to #22—or even to #28, for that matter—will return big dividends to the new tier. It's not something I'd recommend that he begin with when first learning the craft, but after a few months during which he's tied a fair number of flies on hooks in the range of #12 to #16, he should certainly try smaller sizes. A few hours devoted to using gauzy 000000 thread, splitting strands of floss or wool into two or three segments and attaching these materials to hooks of the smallest sizes will increase his ability and confidence when tying on hooks that are larger. After the #22 and #24 hook experience is behind him, no matter how badly his minuscule creations turned out, when he goes back to #12 and #14 hooks he's going to feel as though the 000 thread were sashcord and the #14 hooks ship's anchors. And he'll tie on them with greater skill and speed.

The tying of nymphs and other small flies has been made much easier by the introduction of Monocord, an almost snagless, flat-lying extruded synthetic filament that is very straightforward to handle. In the first series of accompanying pictures, Monocord is being used as ribbing over conventional split floss wrapped on a base of 00000 thread on a #18 Mustad 7948A hook. In spite of the fineness of the materials, it's easy to see how both tying thread and floss spread on the small-diameter wire of the hook shank, while the Monocord retains its shape. The feelers, shown clipped in the last photo, are shown in the next-to-last as they looked when tied in.

This has been a very cursory look at nymphs, which form a large and useful subfamily of wet flies. Nymphs—naturals, that is—are found in almost all streams that hold fish and form an important part of a fish's diet. The few sample dressings in this chapter aren't designed to make you an expert but to give you a working knowledge of tying methods and procedures and a warning of some of the pitfalls to avoid, as well as to encourage you to explore the field further.

Our look at bucktails and streamers in the early pages of the chapter was also cursory but filled in gaps that remained in the chapters on conventional flies insofar as the streamers were concerned. The sum of all these chapters, plus the couple yet to come, will enable you to tackle both streamers and nymphs and might give you some ideas about creating patterns of your own.

Bass Bugs, Poppers, and Saltwater Flies

THESE ARE BIG FLIES for fish who take big bites and are used to eating meat. Bass will tackle almost anything edible; I've fished poppers or bugs in clearwater bass lakes and streams and have seen bass fingerling smaller than the bass bug I was using follow it in to the boat or shore, frantically trying to swallow it. Saltwater fish differ in their eating habits; they aren't insect-gulpers but make their meals off small specimens of their fellows. So we're looking now at an aspect of fly tying in which you'll normally be working on big hooks with big materials.

BASS BUGS AND POPPERS

Oversized flies have been used for bass fishing for a hundred years; the practice goes back so far that nobody quite remembers when it originated. The transition from big flies tied on #2 and #1 hooks to the bodied bug was a logical step, because the bigger the fly, the harder it is to float. None of the angling history I've encountered goes into great detail on the history of the bass bug's creation, and apparently the tier who first noticed how deerhair can be made to flare out on a hook shank remains unknown. By the beginning of the 1900s, cork was beginning to be used as body material for bass bugs, but tiers had trouble constructing cork-bodied bugs in which the body would retain its correct position in relation to the point of the hook. This difficulty persisted until Call J. McCarty invented the hump-shank hook in the early 1900s and earned the gratitude of anglers who like to use a fly rod for their bass fishing.

Poppers didn't begin to appear until the 1930s, and the entire concept of the fly rod as an instrument for the bass fisherman really begins with the development of reliable floating lines shortly after the popper began to gain popularity. New floatable plastics tough enough to withstand the pressure of a bass's strong jaws made smaller versions of the bug and popper practical, and today there are almost as many fly-rod bass fishermen as there are casting-rod anglers.

It would be a mistake, though, to overlook the bug as a very effective means of enticing big trout. One of my most memorable fish was a gigantic brown, one of the unbelievably large trout that in bygone years could be seen almost any day finning below the old wooden bridge that spanned the Merced River's South Fork near the Wawona entrance to Yosemite National Park. A trout fisherman's initiation to Northern California angling wasn't complete then until he'd met these educated browns and joined the army of fishermen they'd frustrated. Occasionally one of the giants would get hooked, but few were landed, because the river's glass-clear water eddying around the bridge piers made gossamer terminal tackle necessary, and these fish knew exactly how to sever a fine leader on the sharp rocks that lined the riverbank at that point.

During World War II, Yosemite was used as a Navy convalescent and rehabilitation center, and local fishermen were invited to teach classes in fly tying and casting, not just to while away long hours for the recuperating battle victims, but to help them regain the manual dexterity they'd lost because of wounds. It was impossible to cross Wawona Bridge without thinking about the trout under it, and on my way to teach a fly-tying class one afternoon I remembered that I had in my kit a bucktail mouse on a #6 hook that I'd tied for the class to use as a model. The temptation was too strong. I stopped and rigged up, using a heavier leader than was possible with a fly.

A false cast or two, and I dropped the mouse just short of the bank across the river from where I stood. It was gulped in after a very short float under the bridge. The trout was big, I had no scales, but my educated guess was that it topped 12 pounds and might have hit 15. That wasn't unusual; at the Yosemite Fish Hatchery the holding pond always contained a few browns of close to 20 pounds, and among the exhibits in the old museum were a pair of browns that weighed 37 and 41 pounds, both taken from the South Fork at Wawona Bridge. There were giants in the river in those days. I had no regret at releasing the big trout, because in my mind I'd discovered the secret that would allow me to come back later and hook the even bigger ones that still hung under the bridge.

Later never came, somehow, and now both bridge and trout are gone, I'm told, from Wawona, but small bucktail bugs in subsequent days have brought me some outstanding trout. The most effective seem to be the mouse and grasshopper patterns on 1X or 2X long hooks, sizes #6 and #8.

These two are the simplest and most productive deerhair bug patterns going, I'm told by angling acquaintances with whom I compare notes. Tying them isn't too complicated, for once you learn to tie a deerhair bug, it's the final trimming of the body that produces the pattern. We'll deal here with the basic bug body.

Begin your deerhair bug by winding tying thread, 00 or A, depending on hook size, from the front of the shank to the bend, then overwinding the thread base forward and back in wide spirals so that the thread crisscrosses. Cut a pinch of hair—deer, antelope, or elk—and comb out the underbody fur. There won't be much, for none of these animals have thick undercoats.

Lay the hair on the hook almost at right angles to the shank and loop the tying thread over it. Holding the hair loosely, pull on the thread, allowing the hair to twist a bit on the hook. As you put pressure on the thread, the hair will flare out from the hook. Help it by pulling the thread down through the flaring hair two or three times at different points, working the thread carefully between the hairs to avoid catching too many and binding them to the hook. This creates gaps in the finished body and makes a loose tie that might not stand up well when cast. If you catch unwanted hair with your thread during this step of the operation, use the bodkin to pull the hairs free before you tighten the thread too much.

When you've finished setting the first pinch of hair, cut a second pinch and clear it of underbody fur. Pull back the hair already flared on the hook and form a very small shoulder in front of it with thread so that it won't get mixed up with the next pinch, which you add in front of the first. Tie it in as closely as possible to the hair put on in the first operation. Repeat this again, and then once more if necessary to fill the hook shank.

When you've tied in all the hair the hook will hold comfortably, tie it off. Your bug will at this point look like a disaster area, but don't let that bother you. It's the trimming that makes a deerhair bug, and you can turn that untidy mass of straggling hair-ends into any of several finished shapes. Many tiers like to tie off the thread with a half hitch or even form the head before trimming, then take the bug out of the vise so that they can turn it easily while they snip. Others leave it in the vise and trim by a combination of looking and feeling. It's probably easier to do the former until you learn how to handle the latter.

Trim with just the tips of your scissors and take off the protruding hair-ends with a lot of small snips instead of trying to do it all with a few quick cuts of the whole blades. Compare both sides of the bug as it takes shape to keep the trimming symmetrical, fix in your mind a picture of the hook shank's position, and remember that it should be in the center of the finished bug.

Trim the body into an egglike shape with a slightly flattened bottom, add a thin, trimmed saddle hackle tail, and your bug is a mouse. Trim the body into a flattened, elongated oval, add a split tail, and you've got a frog. Trim it into a boxy, upright rectangle, and the bug becomes a grasshopper. Of course, you need to plan before you start tying the body and add the appendages of the type of bug you want to wind up with; tie these in as you'd tie in a tail before you begin covering the hook shank with hair.

Tails and legs don't have to be fancy. Don't waste time trying to get a too-exact imitation. Trim a single saddle hackle closely along the quill on both sides to make a mousetail. Make frog legs by whipping long bucktail hairs into a couple of cones, holding them together with tying thread. You can do these jobs in a very few minutes if you don't get caught up by the idea that your objective is to create a totally realistic imitation. That's not the

1. Cut and clean a tuft of deerhair to begin your hair-bodied bug. The hook has been wrapped in the usual way, then overwrapped from back to front and back to the bend in wide spirals to form a criss-cross pattern; this gives the hair a better foundation.

2. Lay the tuft of cleaned hair across the hook almost at right angles and tie in with a loop. Release the hair and tighten the loop; the hair will flare out from the hook. Help it by adding another loop or two, pulling each one very tight.

Tying a
Deerhair Bug

3. Pull back the hair and form a very small shoulder in front of it to encourage it to stay erect.

4. Tie in a second pinch of hair as close in front of the first as you can manage and flare it out from the hook by pressure of the thread as you did the first. Add a third tuft in the same fashion if necessary, and a fourth if required.

5. Trim the untidy mass of straggly hair into the desired body shape, working with the tips of the scissors and taking snips rather than cuts, removing only a small quantity of hair with each snip.

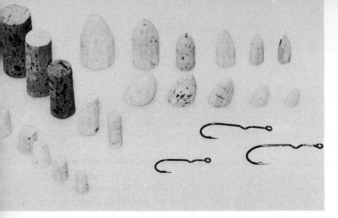

Form your own popper bodies from cork blanks like those at right. Hump-shank hooks like those in the right foreground are necessary to keep the body from twisting around on the hook and throwing the bug off-balance.

idea, all you want to do is imitate the shape of the mouse or frog or whatever the creature may be closely enough to fool a fish speeding toward it with food in mind. Leave total realism to the sculptor or cast plastic lures; you're not sculpting, you're tying flies.

Of course, you can do with cork or plastic bodies just about anything you can with deerhair bodies, but the latter are lighter, easier to cast and feel softer to the taking fish. That softness might give you an extra fraction of a second to set your hook when the fish are striking half-heartedly. But you make the choice, deerhair bugs or bugs with cork or plastic bodies.

The chances are you'll wind up trying both, especially if you like to fish poppers. You can tie poppers with deerhair bodies by slanting the hair at the front when you trim and coating it heavily with head cement to give it water resistance. It's easier to make poppers with cork, or to buy preformed bodies of plastic. There are a lot of these preformed body shapes to select from, including cork cylinders in a size range to fit hooks from #1/0 down to #10. The hump-shank hooks required for solid-bodied flies are available in those sizes, too.

Putting cork-bodied bugs or poppers together is a breeze. The only tying necessary is whipping thread along the humped hook shank and tying on a tail made from three or four saddle hackles or some gaudy fur. After the tail's in place, coat the hook shank generously with a waterproof cement; Pliobond is a good choice, because it dries fairly fast and doesn't have to be clamped or put under pressure to give a good bond. Fit the body over the hook shank; most of the ready-formed bodies you get will have slits already cut. Be sure to fill the slit with glue after the body's fitted in place; the easy way to do this is to turn the bug upside down in the vise, smooth in the adhesive with a cocktail pick, and let it stay there for a few minutes until the glue sets a bit, then lay the glued body aside until it's dry. Paint when the glue dries, and your popper's finished.

You'll save a bit of money if you form your own bodies, and in the early chapters of this book you'll find all the details you need to know about doing this; refer to the chapter on plugs. There are things you can do to dress up your bugs and poppers if you wish. Some tiers add hackle to bugs —not to poppers, since this interferes with their ability to make an appetizing gurgle. Some add a ruff of feathers at the rear of the body instead of, or

Tying a Popping Bug

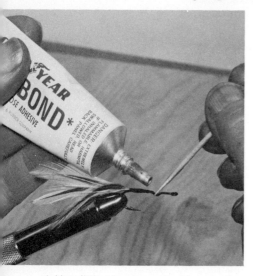

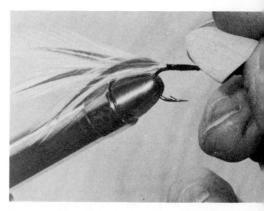

1. Very little tying is required for popping bugs. Cover the hook with thread along the portion the body will occupy and tie in a few saddle hackles or a hair wisp for a tail. Then tie off the thread and clip it, and coat the shank generously with adhesive.

2. Force the slit body over the shank, steadying the hook in the vise with a fingertip under the eye.

3. Turn the bug upside down in the vise and fill the hook slot with adhesive; smooth it and remove excess with a toothpick.

4. When the adhesive has dried, put the popper back in the vise to hold it steady while painting the cork.

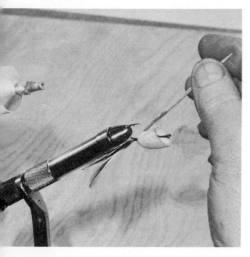

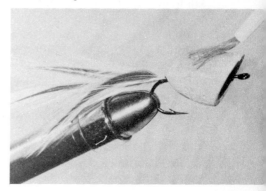

in addition to, hackle. Some drill holes in the sides of the cork body and glue in clipped saddle hackles for wings, or put on hairwings either by tying them around the body or putting them in drilled holes after dipping them in glue. My own preference is to do as little as possible to a bass bug, add a tail or ruff, but stop there. Then go wild with the paint.

There's really not a great deal of work to making bugs and poppers, whether you buy ready-made bodies or form your own. Most of your time is spent waiting for the paint or glue to dry. And don't forget to make a few bugs in small sizes. I kid you not — they have very taking ways with trout.

SALTWATER FLIES

Saltwater flies are usually big because you're going after big fish in most cases, and you need big flies to attract them. You also need, again in most cases, flies that get down quickly and look good to the fish. At the same time, the flies can't be so big and heavy that they're clumsy or impossible to cast with today's modern tackle. The saltwater tier is facing the double challenge of conquering both weight and bulk in his work while producing an effective fly.

Basically there are two types of saltwater flies, one designed to sink fast and go deep, the other to sink slowly and almost hang in the water only a few feet under the surface. The deep-running fly is for deepwater fishing, of course, while the shallow-running, slow sinker finds its place inshore, over spots such as the bonefish flats, and in tidal waters. Then, as distinguished from the big offshore flies, there's a family of smaller flies used by anglers seeking the anadromous fish that move into brackish water to spawn or feed, fish such as striped bass·and tarpon. These small flies include poppers and differ only very slightly from the bigger freshwater bass bugs and bass flies.

A practical limit to the size of hooks on which saltwater flies are dressed would be about 6/0, with the most practical hook sizes being 3/0 and 4/0, from the standpoint of the offshore angler. Shallow-running flies may be dressed on hooks as small as 1/0, but 2/0 and 3/0 hooks are most common. Brackish-water flies are seldom dressed on hooks larger than 2/0, and sizes #1 or 1/0 are more common. Stainless steel ring-eye hooks are the choice of virtually all tiers for the big deepwater jobs, while about half the shallow-running flies are tied on stainless steel TDE hooks, and preference is split about fifty-fifty between TDE stainless and standard bronzed hooks for brackish-water flies and poppers. Long-shanked hooks are used for perhaps half the saltwater flies with which I'm acquainted, and flies dressed extralong to imitate such saltwater food fish as eels often have tandem hooks.

In the materials field, big saddle hackles and imitation polar bear hair predominate, and Mylar piping and tinsel are overwhelmingly the preferred body materials, since Mylar is tarnishproof. Marabou is rarely used; its habit of clinging to hooks while false casts are being made as well as its fragility when exposed to the slashing teeth of saltwater fish take it almost completely out of the picture, though it is used on brackish-water bugs and poppers.

Tying styles vary; few saltwater flies are winged, since the fish they're designed to attract are meat-eaters, not conditioned to snap up such small morsels as insects. Hackle is often omitted from deep-running flies but is a standard on shallow runners, as it helps to achieve the slow sinking and in-water hanging desired by anglers fishing the shallows. Often the hackle is tied just ahead of the bend, and the front of the shank left bare. Tails, usually a bunch of big saddle hackles, are usually tied fairly high on the hook shank to reduce the chance that they'll tangle around the bend and barb.

If we exclude the brackish-water flies and poppers, which are closer kin to the big bass flies used in freshwater, saltwater flies can be divided into about three predominant styles. First in importance is the fly that imitates small food fish, equivalent to the freshwater minnow imitation. Second is the elongated style of tying that imitates the eel. Third is the imitation of the shrimp. We might add a fourth type, equally common in freshwater, the fly that imitates nothing but bears a family resemblance to fish food and attracts the strike by a fish hoping that what he takes is edible.

Tying saltwater flies can be a lot of fun, because you're working with ma-terials scaled up sharply from the small bits and pieces used in tying fresh-water flies. A prototype of the hackled fly might begin with a Mylar tubing body. This material is a braided shell of silvery plastic strips over a core of cotton cording, and the core must be removed after a piece of the tubing has been measured against the length of the hook shank and cut off. If you're cutting Mylar tubing for several flies of the same size, wrap a strip of narrow masking tape at each cut-off point and cut through the center of the tape to keep the braiding from unraveling. The braiding stretches, so take this into account when measuring.

Use tweezers or hackle pliers to pull out the cotton coring, and after wrapping on your tying thread—usually size A to D, depending on the hook—and setting the tail, slip the tubing over the hook eye and down the shank. Tie in above any frayed ends, and finish with a whip finish. Push the tubing back from the eye of the hook and start the tying thread with an overwrap, then pull the tubing forward and tie it off, again working above the frayed end where the braid's strands have separated. Tie in two or three or more large saddle hackles, wrap them, and head off the fly.

To tie the deep-running fly, omit the hackling, but if you wish, put on a wing bucktail-style, using imitation polar bear hair or some other iridescent material such as karakul. Mylar is available in sheeting as well as tubing and tinsel, and a small square can be fringed with scissors, leaving a collar along one edge for tying. Cut the fringe fairly wide so that it will hold up under sharp-toothed attacks. Attach the fringed piece of Mylar around the shank just below the head in the fashion of wet-fly hackle.

Pay special attention to saltwater fly heads. Give them not just one or two, but four or five coats of head lacquer; the large-diameter thread isn't as

Tying a Saltwater Fly

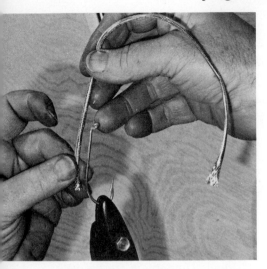

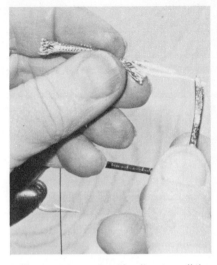

1. Measure Mylar piping for length along the shank of the hook you will use. The hook in the vise is a #6/0 Mustad 3408B.

2. Use tweezers or hackle pliers to pull the cotton core out of the Mylar piping.

4. Smooth the tubing on the hook shank, tie in at the tail above any frayed loose ends of the piping and trim off the frayed bits after tying in. Cover the end of the piping with thread and tie off with a whip-finish. Cut the tying thread; apply head cement generously to the wrap.

3. After wrapping the hook and tying in a tail of saddle hackles, slip the piping on over the eye.

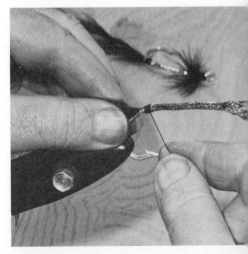

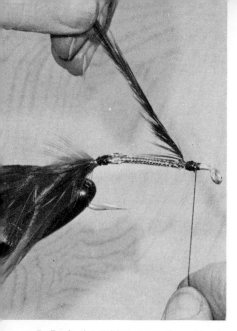

5. Push the tubing back from the eye along the shank and start your tying thread again behind the eye. Pull the piping forward and tie in behind the frayed portion; trim away loose ends of piping as before. Wrap the end of the tubing, tie in and wrap several big saddle hackles, tie off and head the fly.

6. This is a typical pattern for a midwater or shallow-running saltwater fly, designed to sink slowly and maintain position without seeking greater depth.

easy to coat as the smaller threads used on freshwater hooks; it drinks head cement like a toper.

Tying the eel imitation involves the same technique given in an earlier chapter in Part I of the book; you're simply making a surge tube lure with a couple of hackles tied in streamer-style at the head.

Tying the shrimp imitation duplicates the process given in the preceding chapter where the hardback nymph is detailed. The only difference is that instead of a quill fiber strip being used to form the back, a pinch of hair is indicated for the shrimp fly. The tying steps are the same. Tie in the material for the back; I like brown squirreltail hair for this. Form the body of chenille, pink or cream; if you wish, tie a saddle-hackle Palmer along the hook shank and when wrapping the chenille, let the hackle fibers protrude below the chenille in patches to imitate legs. Bring the hair up over the body after it's formed and tie off the hair so that it spreads over the top of the chenille body.

If you can tie freshwater flies on small hooks, you can certainly tie saltwater flies on big hooks without suffering any pain.

14

Traditional
Fly Patterns

THIS CHAPTER DOESN'T PRETEND to offer a definitive or complete listing of all fly patterns. Nobody really knows how many patterns there actually are, because everywhere that anglers fish with flies there are local patterns unknown outside that immediate vicinity. And every day of every fishing season, an unknown, unknowable number of fly-tying anglers create new patterns. This process has been going on for several centuries, so there are certainly hundreds of patterns that never got to the point of being listed in books such as this one. Conversely old fly patterns never die, once they get listed; fishermen stop using them, but the patterns keep on being listed.

After having tied a quite astronomical number of flies and having discussed the art for several decades with scores of other tiers, I've just about concluded that the precise duplication of a fly pattern is more an accident than it is a matter of purposeful knowledge. Think about it for a moment, and I believe you'll agree. There are simply too many variables between the eye and the written or spoken word. No matter how minutely a fly pattern is described, one man's "light" is another man's "medium" shade; one man's "bright" is another's "pale," and so on. There are also a lot of variations in the types and shades of dyes used on tying materials, as well as in materials such as wool or chenille or silk that react differently to dyes of the same shade. How many tones of scarlet or blue or claret or brown can you pin down with words?

Every angler who ties and fishes flies has had experiences similar to mine in switching from one batch of material to another. We've found that some variation either in the dye or the refraction index of the material itself has reduced the attractiveness of that material to the eyes of the fish. Flies tied with old materials of the same shade and type still produce; flies tied with new materials supposedly identical fail to produce. To the human eye the color and appearance may be the same, but they don't look the same to a fish.

166

Does this mean that color's more important than shape? Not necessarily. Does it mean that shape's more important, then? Again, not necessarily. Quite some years ago, Walt Thoreson, for whom Jim Pray named the Thor fly, gave me several Thors that Pray had tied before his death. I'd been taking fish regularly with Thor flies I'd tied, and so had other anglers I knew. But when we compared our Thors with those tied by Pray, there were several different shades of color and several different body configurations that could be seen at a glance.

Not even the most skilled and knowledgeable professional fly tiers are in unanimous agreement on patterns. It's quite possible for several of them to remain within the limits of a pattern and still produce several different versions of the same fly, all versions equally authentic. Factors like this, though, keep the compiler of pattern lists from being dogmatic.

There are, of course, legitimate variations in fly patterns. These are usually limited — or should be limited — to minor changes such as a choice between wool or fur dubbing of the same shade, the addition or subtraction of a tag or tip, or a changed style of setting the wings. These don't destroy the integrity of a fly pattern. Any fly can be dressed to be fished wet or dry, and many can be dressed as streamers. Dry flies can be tied with variant hackle or Palmer hackle, or as bivisibles, without losing their identity, though I suspect that some of these changes will alter the fly's attraction to the fish.

However, there's a point of no return in making changes in dressings and in changing fly names; in fact, there are two points of no return representing opposite ends of the scale of changes. Logically, if you begin with a fly that includes six kinds of materials in a scheme of four colors and change five of the materials and three of the colors, any resemblance to the original has been lost. Adding a number, calling the changed fly the "Oscar Wimbish Special #5" can't create a kinship with its original dressing. It's like mixing a cocktail with vodka and dry Vermouth and calling it a Martini. A Martini is made with gin; substituting vodka makes it a different drink which is entitled to its own identity and shouldn't traffic on the Martini's good name.

On the reverse end of the scale, if you take a fly pattern that's been around a few decades, includes six kinds of materials in a scheme of four colors, and make one minor change in its dressing, you haven't created a new fly. Putting your name on it is like substituting your own picture for that of George Washington on a dollar bill. Either of these two extremes is illegitimate, yet you'll find them reflected on a lot of fly pattern lists.

Take a couple of weeks off sometime and analyze a list of three thousand fly patterns and your findings will agree with mine. Fewer than a third of them are unduplicated creations. Carry your analysis a bit further and you'll find that 80 percent of the remaining patterns are either regional, seasonal, or specialized. They're flies that are terrific in a ten-mile stretch of the Lower Squawtash River on either side of Podunk Corners, or in that little lake just outside of Twotoe Junction, but elsewhere they won't take fish one. Or, they're flies guaranteed to produce the third week in June in a limited geographical area, but just try taking a fish on them in September. Or, they're flies over which an Atlantic salmon or a Florida bass goes ape, but at which a trout in the Rockies or Sierras turns up its nose.

About half the remaining 20 percent almost make up the grade as flies for all waters regardless of geography for all seasons, and all fish regardless of species. Granted that fish are finicky, a lot of this is due to fishermen pampering them. The angler goes to the stream or lake thinking, "Now, there's no use trying anything but a Passionate Purple Poddlewoggle today, because that's all the fish will take here at this time of the year." Well, he might be right; there are waters and seasons that demand specific flies at specific times. I strongly suspect that the range of such waters is narrower and the seasons longer than most fishermen believe, though. I've taken a lot of fish on flies that local anglers swore wouldn't work.

All this, of course, is leading up to the fly lists that follow. They're short, and perhaps contain some surprising patterns. But, they're the closest I can come to a list of all-purpose, all-season, all-area flies. Not all of them will meet all three criteria, but if you're beginning as a tyer, these will get you off to a good start. There's a certain amount of personal experiences — prejudice, if you want to call it that — reflected in the lists. For instance, I usually do better fishing the Coachman wet than dry, and do better with a dry Royal Coachman fishing for bass than for trout. Don't let that stop you from reversing my pattern of using them, because you might do right something I've been doing wrong.

Please don't get the impression that because this list is so limited, I'm implying in compiling it that other flies don't have a place in your box. They do; I carry and use a lot of other patterns on specific streams and lakes at specific seasons. If you want to consult more complete pattern lists, there are lots of them around. Look up the books on fly tying by such fellows as Edson Leonard, A. J. McClane, Vincent Marinaro, Ray Bergman, Art Flick, Rex Gerlach, Joe Brooks, and many others. Ernest Schwiebert's book on nymphs is outstanding. Kenneth Bay has in a recent book begun the job of codifying patterns for saltwater flies.

Enjoy tying, enjoy fishing, and may you never cast wind knots into your leader.

FLY PATTERNS

Note: Unless specified, dubbing may be fur or wool. Unless specified, all tippets are from golden pheasant. Unless specified, all herl is peacock. Unless specified, colors may be either natural or dyed.

Popular Fly
Patterns

TROUT DRY FLIES

PATTERN	TAG	TAIL	TIP	RIB-BING	BODY	WINGS	HACKLE	NOTES
BADGER		Light badger			Grey wool		Light badger Palmer	Alternate dressing: quill body, grizzly tail.
BEAVERKILL QUILL					White and brown quill (condor)	Mallard	Brown	Alternate dressings: female, add yellow chenille butt; body can be floss or wool tied in stripes.
BLACK GNAT	Gold				Black herl	Black hackle tips		Alternate dressings: chenille or wool; red tail infrequently added
BLUEBOTTLE			Gold	Gold	Blue floss	Black	Black	
BLUE QUILL		Blue dun hackle wisps			Peacock herl	Medium grey	Blue dun	Alternate dressings: Body, light and dark moose mane, striped.
BLUE DUN		Blue dun hackle wisps			Pale blue dubbed fur	Pale grey	Pale blue dun	Alternate dressings: grey wool body; tie as wet with silver tinsel body.
CAHILL (DARK)		Wood duck	Gold		Yellowish-grey fur dubbing	Wood duck	Brown	Alternate dressings: (light) cream fur dubbing body; gold tinsel body; lemon floss body, ginger hackle; peacock quill body, brown hackle; black thread rib on light bodies.

FLY PATTERNS

Note: Unless specified, dubbing may be fur or wool. Unless specified, all tippets are from golden pheasant. Unless specified, all herl is peacock. Unless specified, colors may be either natural or dyed.

	Tail	Body	Rib	Tip	Wing	Hackle	Alternate dressings
CROSS SPECIAL	Wood duck	Cream fur dubbing			Wood duck	Blue dun	
GINGER QUILL	Ginger	Dark quill			Dark grey	Ginger	Alternate dressings: wood duck wings; grey wings; ginger hackle tip wings; wingless, Palmer hackle.
GOLD-RIBBED HARE'S EAR		Hare's ear fur dubbing, picked	Gold	Gold	Grey		Alternate dressings: brown tail and wings; rabbit hair tail; rarely, brown hackle. Try poly-wool on this pattern.
GREY HACKLE	Red hackle wisps	Herl		Gold		Grizzly	Alternate dressings: as many as there body materials; this is a family of flies, the body color determining the name, as Grey Hackle Red, etc. It is one of several hackle fly families, and the only one that's been much good for me fished dry.
IRON BLUE DUN	Iron blue dun hackle wisps	Brown and deep red dubbing			Coot	Iron blue dun	Alternate dressings: grey dubbing body, gold tip; coch-y-bondhu hackle, red floss tip; iron blue dun body; peacock herl quill body; blue quill body; tier's choice of hackle in alternate dressings, brown, grizzly or olive brown.
MOSQUITO		Black thread quill			Grizzly hackle tips, spent	Grizzly (sparse)	Alternate dressings: white or grey floss body, very thin. This is a poly-yarn natural, omit hackle when using this yarn. Use #14 or smaller hook.
SPIDER		Brown floss				Grizzly	Use special hook, see text.

171

TROUT WET FLIES

PATTERN	TAG	TAIL	TIP	RIB-BING	BODY	WINGS	HACKLE	NOTES
BLACK JUNE			Gold	Silver	Herl	Dark grey	Black, full	Alternate dressings: black wings. If tied with a black floss body, fly is called Black May. Fish shallow to mid-water.
BROWN HACKLE	Gold	Pheasant tippet			Herl		Brown, full	Alternate dressings: any body material; this is a family in which body color gives the fly its name: Brown Hackle Red, etc. Floss, wool and dubbing are used about equally in bodies. Fish at any depth.
COACHMAN	Gold	Pheasant tippet			Herl	White	Brown, throat	Alternate dressings: over the years, so many alternates have been evolved that this old and excellent fly has almost lost its original identity. The original pattern is more productive than any alternate I've tried.
COWDUNG			Gold		Greenish-yellow wool	Grey	Brown, throat	Alternate dressings: dark olive or orange wool; ginger wings and hackle.
DUSTY MILLER		Brown feather fibers	Gold		Grey dubbing	Grey	Grizzly, full, but sparse	Alternate dressings: grey turkey tail, grey mohair body, gold rib. Fish mid-water to shallow.

GREY HACKLE: See pattern in dry fly listing; tie with full hackle.

							Notes
IMPROVED GOVERNOR	Gold	Red hackle wisps	Gold, narrow over floss	1/3 herl fore, 2/3 red floss aft	Brown	Brown, throat	Alternate dressings: the original pattern, herl body with red floss tip.
JOE O'DONNELL		Red hackle tip		Cream chenille, fat	Badger hackle tips, jungle cock eye	Mixed red & yellow, full	Alternate dressings: gold (oval) tinsel body. Originated for steelhead. Originated on big hooks, good midwater to deep stream fly on #10 and #12 hooks.
LADY BUG			Gold, narrow	Red wool	Grey, tied as case over back	Brown, as feelers	Alternate dressings: orange wool body. See text for detailed dressing. Fish very shallow, just under surface.
MARCH BROWN	Gold	Brown	Yellow floss	Tan dubbing	Brown turkey	Brown, throat	Alternate dressings: tied as dry fly, becomes Dun Drake.
PROFESSOR		Scarlet	Gold	Yellow floss	Mallard	Brown, throat	Alternate dressing: orange body, grozzly hackle. Fish midwater to deep.
ROYAL COACHMAN	Gold	Pheasant tippet		Herl, scarlet center joint 1/3	White	Brown, throat	Alternate dressings: (leadwing) slate wings; (Wulff) white hair wings.
TREE ANT				Black chenille, waisted	Black, looped at waist, narrow		See text for full details of tying. Fish deep.
WOOLY WORM		Red		Black chenille, full		Badger, Palmer	Alternate dressings: red, brown or yellow body. Fish deep.

TROUT STREAMER FLIES

PATTERN	TAG	TAIL	TIP	RIB-BING	BODY	WINGS	HACKLE	NOTES
ADIRONDACK		Yellow		Gold	Tan wool	White	Orange, throat	Alternate dressings: (Scarlet) red wool body and tail, brown wings, scarlet hackle; scarlet dressing + gold tag turns fly into Admiral. Tie on 2x or 3x hook.
EDISON TIGER		Wood duck	Silver		Yellow chenille	Brown bucktail, herl topping, jungle cock eye	Red, throat	Alternate dressings: (Light) herl body, yellow bucktail wing. 3x hook.
R. B. FIERY		Pheasant tippet	Gold	Gold	Fiery brown wool	Brown bucktail	Grizzly, throat	Alternate dressings: (standard) gold & brown wool body, bronze turkey wing, Rhode Island Red rooster wing. There's nothing wrong with the standard dressing, but Bergman's has been better for me. Tie on 3x hook.
GRAY GHOST				Silver	Orange floss	Dun neck hackle, silver pheasant shoulder, jungle cock eye	Yellow over herl over white, throat	Alternate dressings: short orange wool tail. 3x hook. One of the most effective trout streamers.
HIGHLAND BELLE				Silver	Gold	Grizzly over orange saddle hackles	White hair, throat	No alternates. This is a streamer version of a standard salmon fly. 3x or 4x hook.

	TAG	TAIL	TIP	RIB-BING	BODY	WINGS	HACKLE	NOTES
LADY GHOST		Pheasant tippet		Silver narrow oval	Silver, wide flat	Badger saddle hackles, pheasant crest topping	Herl & white hair mixed, throat	Tie of 3x hook.
MUDDLER MINNOW		Grey hair			Gold	Brown turkey over black & white hair	Bucktail, trimmed	No alternates. Tie hackle in thin strip, trim to form rounded collar. 3x pr 4x hook. To tie dry, use wider hackle and trim longer than for wet.
SWIFT-WATER		Grey			Herl, orange wool center joint	White turkey	Brown	Alternate dressing: omit joint. 4x hook. Don't be led by name to use only in streams, an excellent lake fly.

BASS DRY FLIES

PATTERN	TAG	TAIL	TIP	RIB-BING	BODY	WINGS	HACKLE	NOTES
BUTCHER		Scarlet		Yellow floss	Scarlet floss		Grizzly dyed yellow, Palmer	Alternate patterns: dark red body & hackle; grey or blue wings, full but not Palmered red hackle.
COLONEL		Yellow & black		Gold	Yellow floss	Yellow, red splits	Yellow	Alternate dressings: scarlet tail.

BASS DRY FLIES

PATTERN	TAG	TAIL	TIP	RIB-BING	BODY	WINGS	HACKLE	NOTES
DEERHAIR BUG		Bucktail wisp			Dearhair, trimmed oval			Alternate dressings: deerhair wings, short. Tie any color, or use natural antelope for lighter body, elk for darker body. Fish slowly, let it lie on water and twitch occasionally.
DEERHAIR GRASS-HOPPER					Light tan dearhair, trimmed			Trim hair into narrow rectangle, add wisps to suggest wings. See text.
HARLEQUIN BUG		Scarlet bucktail wisps			Dyed deer-hair, ½ red fore, ½ blue aft	Yellow		Trim hair in tapered cylinder, short wings. 3x to 6x hook. Fish slowly.
LORD BALTI-MORE		Black		Black floss	Orange floss	Black, spoon	Black	Spoon wings. Jungle cock eye often added.
McGINTY		Scarlet			Yellow chenille, black chenille joint	White tipped mallard	Brown	Alternate dressings: body tied ¼ black and yellow chenille, fly then called Bee.
MUDDLER MINNOW		White fur		Silver, round	Gold, flat	Brown turkey over black & white hair	Bucktail, trimmed	Tie on 4x to 6x long hook; trim hackle long—about ½ on 4x hook.

PATTERN	TAG	TAIL	TIP	RIB-BING	BODY	WINGS	HACKLE	NOTES
RIO GRANDE KING	Gold, wide	Yellow			Black chenille	White, spoon	Yellow	Alternate dressing: red tail.
ROYAL COACH-MAN	Gold	Pheasant tippet			Herl, red floss joint	White	Brown	There are many alternates, none as effective as the original. In my book, more effective as a dry fly for bass than for trout.

BASS WET FLIES

PATTERN	TAG	TAIL	TIP	RIB-BING	BODY	WINGS	HACKLE	NOTES
BRASS HAT		Yellow			Brass wire	Black over yellow over white hair		Another steelhead fly that turns out to good for bass. Fish deep and fast.
DOLLY VARDEN		Cinnamon		Gold	White floss	Cinnamon	Brown	Alternate pattern: silver body.
GRIZZLY KING		Scarlet		Gold	Green dubbing	Grey mallard	Grizzly, full	Alternate dressing: Green floss body, red splits.
INDIAN FLY		Red			Red & yellow wool		Red, full	Tie body fat, the wool should be large diameter, tied in alternate stripes.
PERCH FLY				Gold	White floss	Yellow, red & white strips	Yellow, throat	Dress with a long spoon wing, closed.
PINK LADY	Gold	Ginger		Gold	Pink floss	Mallard	Ginger, full	Fish very slow and shallow.

BASS WET FLIES

PATTERN	TAG	TAIL	TIP	RIB-BING	BODY	WINGS	HACKLE	NOTES
RED FOX	Gold	Lemon-yellow			Pale fox belly fur dubbing	Grey	Brown, full	Another Ray Bergman winner; fish shallow and slow.
SCARLET IBIS		Scarlet		Gold	Scarlet	Scarlet	Scarlet, full	Bass must be part bull; they hit on red over any other color.
THOR		Orange			Maroon floss	White polar bear hair	Brown hair, throat	Jim Pray created this for steelhead, but it's equally inviting to bass.
WHITE MILLER	Orange floss				White chenille	White, spoon	White, throat	Most effective fished midwater in warm water lakes and slow streams.

BASS STREAMER FLIES

PATTERN	TAG	TAIL	TIP	RIB-BING	BODY	WINGS	HACKLE	NOTES
BLACK DEMON		Silver pheasant			Silver, oval	Black hair	Badger, throat	2x to 4x hook.
BLACK GHOST		Yellow		Silver	Black floss	4 white saddle hackles	Yellow, throat	4x to 6x hook.

Name	Tail	Body	Rib	Wing	Hackle	Remarks
CAIN RIVER	Pheasant crest wisps	Gold, oval		Yellow over red saddle hackles	Yellow, blue front, throat	2x or 3x hook.
MARABOU SPECIAL	Pheasant tippet	Silver, flat		White marabou, pintail sides		Fish very slowly for best action.
MICKEY FINN		Silver, flat	Silver, twisted	Yellow over red over yellow hair		A good bass-finder; fish slow with short jerky retrieve.
OPTIC RED		Gold, oval		Red polar bear hair	Brass bead	Pray's Optic flies form a family that's attractive to both steelhead and bass; they sink deeply, so retrieve fairly fast to avoid bottom hangups.
ORLEANS BARBER	Red	Red chenille			Grizzly saddles, long, ½ Palmer	Holds well in shallow and midwater.
POWDER PUFF					Red marabou, about 6 short feathers tied around eye	Fish slow with pumping retrieve.
REUBEN WOOD	Red Grey	White chenille		Mallard, spent	Brown	One of the earliest and still one of the best bass flies.
ROGUE	Red	Green chenille	Silver	White polar bear hair	Grizzly, throat	Steelhead retread, use 4x or 6x hook.

Supply Sources

There are several types of supply sources for lure-making and fly-tying equipment and materials. They include those you've heard about but never tried, those you've tried and found wanting, and those from whom you've gotten good service and satisfactory merchandise over a period of years, and I've confined this list to the last group. There's also another category of suppliers, those whose business isn't primarily fishing equipment and materials, but who have tools that are hard to find elsewhere or materials that can be used in lure making that you might not find in a tackle supplier's catalog. A couple of the firms on the following list fall into this group.

Appalachian Angler Box 216 Smyrna, GA 30080	Fly tying tools and supplies
Brookstone Co. Peterborough, N H 03458	Metal and woodworking tools, special adhesives, tapes
Carolina Novelty Co. 2412 Kenmore Avenue Charlotte, N C 28204	Lure components, molds for casting plastic and metal, hooks
Finnysports 2910 Glanzman Road Toledo, OH 43614	Complete line of lure-making and fly-tying tools and supplies
Herter's Route 2 Mitchell, S D 57301	Complete line of lure-making and fly-tying tools and supplies
E. Hille Box 269 Williamsport, PA 17701	Complete line of lure-making and fly-tying tools and supplies
Limit Manufacturing Corp. Box 367 Richardson, TX 75080	Molds and casting materials, lure-making components, fly-tying tools
Midland Tackle Co. 66 Route 17 Sloatsburg, NY 10974	Complete line of lure-making and fly-tying tools and supplies
Netcraft Co. 3101 Sylvania Avenue Toledo, OH 43613	Complete line of lure-making and fly-tying tools and supplies
Ojai Fisherman 218 North Encinal Ave. Ojai, CA 93023	Fly-tying tools and supplies
Rangely Region Sports Shop 28 Main Street Rangely, ME 04970	• Fly-tying tools and supplies
Reed Tackle Co. Box 390 Caldwell, N J 07006	Complete line of lure-making and fly-tying tools and supplies
S&K Tackle Co. 857 Butler Street Toledo, OH 43605	Molds and casting materials, lure-making components, hooks
J. C. Whitney Co. Box 8410 Chicago, ILL 60680	Metalworking tools, adhesives, finishes, tapes, metal items from which lures can be made

As you'll note, not all these firms carry full lines of all the things you'll need for lures and flies. Some specialize, and as a result you'll find more items in their catalogs in these special lines. However, where the word "complete" is used, it means just that.

Index